THE LINE

THE LINE

A Story of Excellence in the Margins

JAKE THOMPSON

The Line: A Story of Excellence in the Margins

Published by Clovercroft Publishing, Franklin, Tennessee

Interior Layout Design by Suzanne Lawing

Printed in the United States of America

ISBN: 978-1-968127-16-9 (print)

To my wife for her unconditional support along this journey.

To my parents for always encouraging me to compete for my dreams, no matter how big they were.

To my extended family for rooting me on during my journey.

To my JMS and JHS coaches who taught me to compete, lead, and take on challenges.

To my clients, Compete Every Day community, and friends who have supported every step from the trunk of my car to today.

Thank you for believing in me, encouraging me, and holding me accountable to always touch the line when no one was watching.

Acknowledgments

This story—and the lessons within—wouldn't have been possible without the coaches and mentors who poured into me over the years.

To my high school coaches and the lifelong lessons they invested in teaching me through the best game on earth: Danny Long, Matt Turner, Kurt Traylor, Steve Gideon, Clint Harper, Herb Minyard, Clint Barr, and the Jacksonville ISD coaches.

To Tony Vining, who spent the summer before and after his senior year of high school tossing footballs with an undersized future quarterback and inspiring me that you could be under six feet tall and still win.

To Akeem, my fellow QB and one of the best leaders of young men I know. I appreciate your support over the years and continually believing in Compete Every Day (CED). It's fun watching you empower the next generation of players.

To Phil, for helping unlock this framework and sparking a fresh direction in my journey to helping others learn to better compete every day.

To my teammates, friends, and all of those who gave me grace, patience, and encouragement along this journey from immature kid to who I am today.

Thank you.

Dear Competitor,

In addition to the story that you're about to read, I've created a number of additional resources to help you meet *The Line* in life, many of them at zero-cost. Find these resources and more at www.GoTheExtraInch.com.

I'm glad you're here, let's get to work.

- Jake Thompson

CONTENTS

PROLOGUE
THE LINE

The spring air in Jackson Creek, Texas, carried the scent of fresh-cut grass and possibility. The football field at Jackson Creek High School stood empty except for one figure—a sophomore boy with shoulders not yet grown into his frame but eyes that burned with determination—running sprint after sprint in the fading afternoon light.

Barrett "Bear" Wilson bent down, hands on his knees, sweat dripping from his forehead onto the white chalk line at the far hash mark. His lungs burned. He'd been at it for almost an hour now, long after the organized team workouts had ended. The rest of his teammates were already home, probably playing video games or texting girls.

Bear straightened up and looked at the empty bleachers, imagining them filled with screaming fans come fall. Next season would be different. Next season, he wouldn't be stuck on the sidelines watching Tyler Greene—the naturally gifted junior with the rocket arm—lead the Panthers. Next season, he'd find a way to contribute, to compete.

He knew the odds were stacked against him. Where Tyler could flick his wrist and send a perfect spiral 60 yards downfield, Bear had to put his whole body into the same throw. Where Tyler's feet moved with natural quickness that scouts drooled over, Bear had trained relentlessly just to achieve adequate mobility. What Bear lacked in raw talent, though, he made up for in preparation, in understanding the game, in disciplined execution of fundamentals.

But was that enough?

Bear lined up for one more sprint, pushing himself harder, faster. The burning in his muscles had transformed into a dull ache. He was exhausted, but he'd promised himself ten full-speed sprints, touching the far hash mark each time before turning back.

As he reached that mark on his final sprint, he felt his legs giving out. The line lay just before him. No one was watching. No one would know if he cut it short by just those few inches.

Just this once, he thought.

Bear turned early, a few inches shy of the line, and sprinted back toward his starting point. That's when he heard the admonition: "Son, you just cheated yourself."

The voice came from nowhere—deep, commanding but not unkind. Bear nearly tripped, stumbling to a stop and turning to see a man standing at the edge of the field. He was tall, broad-shouldered, around forty, with the weathered look of someone who spent most of his time outdoors.

"I'm sorry?" Bear managed to say between heavy breaths.

The man walked onto the field with the easy confidence of someone who belonged there. "That line," he said, pointing to the hash mark Bear was supposed to touch. "You didn't touch it."

Bear felt heat creep into his face that had nothing to do with the Texas sun. "I'm just tired, sir. Been out here a while."

The man nodded, considering this. "I know. I've been watching you. You've got heart, pushing yourself after practice like this." He paused, his eyes taking Bear's measure. "But that's exactly when touching the line matters most."

Bear felt a mix of embarrassment and irritation. Who was this guy to tell him he was cheating himself? He'd been working hard, harder than anyone else on the team. The idea of touching the line every time seemed excessive, almost obsessive. But something in the man's eyes made him pause. Was there really more to this than he realized?

Suddenly, Bear recognized who he was talking to, and his embarrassment doubled. "You're Tony Brewer."

It wasn't a question. Everyone in Jackson Creek knew Tony Brewer, the hometown hero who'd led Jackson Creek to their only state championship twenty-five years ago. His jersey hung in the school trophy case alongside newspaper headlines proclaiming, "Brewer's Last-Second TD Brings State Glory to Jackson Creek."

Tony smiled, and said, "And you're Barrett Wilson. Coach Turner mentioned you've been working hard."

"Yes sir," Bear said, standing a little straighter despite his fatigue. "But everyone calls me Bear."

"Bear," Tony repeated, testing out the name. "Tell me something, Bear. You know what separates the good from the great?"

Bear thought for a moment. "Talent?"

Tony laughed, but it wasn't unkind. "That's what most people think. But no. The difference is in the details—the small choices that no one sees."

He walked to the hash mark and pointed to it.

"It's that extra inch. The inch between almost and actually. The inch between close enough and excellence."

Bear looked at the line, those few inches he'd skipped suddenly seeming much more significant.

"That line represents a choice," Tony continued. "And choices become habits. Habits become character. And character—" He paused, looking at Bear intently. "Character becomes destiny."

Tony gestured toward the hash mark. "Want to try that sprint again?"

Something about the way he said it made Bear realize it wasn't really a question.

Bear nodded, jogged back to his starting point, and took off again with whatever energy he had left. This time, when he reached the hash mark, he bent down and deliberately touched the white line with his hand before turning and sprinting back.

When he finished, Tony was smiling again.

"Better," he said. "Much better."

"Thanks," Bear managed to say, still catching his breath.

"You heading home?" Tony asked, glancing at the setting sun.

Bear nodded. "My mom's probably wondering where I am. She worries."

"Teachers often do," Tony said with a knowing smile. "Ellen Wilson teaches middle school English, right? I think she taught my nephew a few years back."

"Yes, sir," Bear confirmed, surprised Tony knew his mother.

"And your dad runs Wilson Auto Supply downtown?"

"Yes, sir, all my life." Bear added.

Tony nodded. "Small town. Everyone knows everyone."

He studied Bear for a moment longer, as if making a decision. "Listen, I should let you go. But if you're serious about improving—about getting that extra inch in everything you do—I might be able to help."

"Really?" Bear couldn't keep the eagerness from his voice.

"Meet me at the old Arrington Hardware store downtown at seven a.m. on Saturday." Tony started walking backward toward the parking lot. "Don't be late. Every minute counts."

"I'll be there," Bear called after him. "And . . . thank you, sir."

Tony gave a small wave and turned away, leaving Bear standing alone on the field, staring at the hash mark he'd finally touched properly. As the evening shadows lengthened across the turf, he couldn't shake the feeling that this brief encounter might mean more than he realized.

Little did he know how that single line—and the extra inch of effort required to touch it—would come to reshape not just his football career but also his understanding of what it truly meant to compete in life.

CHAPTER 1
THE BACKUP

Bear's alarm blared at 5 a.m., a full hour before he needed to be at school for morning workouts. He'd been setting it this early for months now, using the quiet predawn hours for film study, mechanics work, and playbook memorization. Despite all that effort, Tyler Greene's name still sat comfortably at the top of the depth chart after spring ball, with Bear's firmly in the second spot.

He dressed quickly in the dark, careful not to make too much noise. His parents were still asleep, though his father would be up soon to open the auto parts store. Bear liked these quiet mornings—the house to himself, the town still slumbering, with nothing but his goals and the day ahead to look forward to.

In the kitchen, he fixed a protein shake and a bowl of oat-meal, eating at the counter while reviewing plays from the team's playbook. He'd practically memorized every formation, every route, every protection scheme. Knowledge wasn't his problem. It was execution—the physical gifts that seemed to come so naturally to Tyler but required constant grinding for Bear.

His father had always told him, "There are two kinds of quarterbacks—those born with a golden arm and those who build one through ten thousand throws." Bear knew which category he fell into.

At 5:45 a.m., he grabbed his backpack and headed out, the spring morning still dark and cool.

The high school was just a mile from his house, an easy drive in his old pickup—a hand-me-down Ford his father had helped him fix up for his sixteenth birthday.

The weight room was already unlocked when he arrived—Coach Turner made sure it was available for the "early birds," as he called them. Bear was usually the first one there, but today he found Tyler already working through a set of bench presses.

"Morning," Bear said, setting down his bag.

Tyler nodded, finishing his rep before sitting up. "Wilson. You're here early."

"Always am," Bear replied, trying to keep the edge from his voice. It wasn't Tyler's fault he'd been born with a cannon for an arm and the quick feet of a running back. "Just usually the only one."

Tyler wiped his face with a towel. "Coach wants me to work on upper body strength. Says my deep ball needs more zip."

Bear almost laughed. Tyler's deep ball already had more zip than Bear could generate with perfect mechanics. If Tyler improved his arm strength even more, what hope did Bear have of competing?

"Cool," was all Bear said, moving to the squat rack to begin his own routine.

They worked out in relative silence, sharing the weight room but following their own programs. By 6:30 a.m., other players began filtering in for the official morning workout.

Coach Turner arrived at exactly 6:45, a clipboard in one hand and a coffee in the other. The head coach was a compact, muscular man in his mid-forties with close-cropped grey hair and perpetually narrowed eyes, as if always assessing, calculating, planning.

"Listen up," he called, and the chatter immediately ceased. "Last day of spring ball. After today, it's on you to maintain what we've built until summer conditioning starts. Time to see which of you will choose to improve on your own time and which will choose to backslide."

His eyes scanned the room, lingering momentarily on Bear before moving on.

"Today we're running installation and situational work. First-team offense against first-team defense. Second teams on the other field."

Bear felt the familiar weight of disappointment. Second team. Again. Despite all the extra hours, all the film study, all the mechanical refinements, he was still looking up at Tyler on the depth chart.

The morning walk-through was crisp and efficient. Bear led the second-team offense against the first-team defense, trying to execute against a unit that knew all their plays and tendencies.

"Wilson! Push it!" Coach Turner barked as Bear hesitated on a read. "Make a decision and live with it!"

Bear dropped back on the next play, scanning the field. The defense had covered his primary and secondary receivers. The pocket was collapsing. He tucked the ball and ran, picking up 8 yards before sliding safely.

"Not bad," Coach Turner said, but Bear could hear the unspoken "but not great" hanging in the air.

After practice, as the other players headed to the locker room, Bear lingered on the field, working on his footwork in the pocket. He repeated his 1-, 2-, 3-, and 5-step drops over and over, focusing on keeping his base solid, his eyes downfield.

"You're still dropping your elbow on your five-step," came Coach Turner's voice from behind him. Bear turned to find the coach watching him, clipboard now tucked under his arm.

"Sorry, Coach. I'll fix it."

"You're working hard, Wilson," Coach said, approaching Bear. "But Greene's still ahead of you."

Bear racked his brain for a diplomatic way to ask the question that had been eating at him all spring. Finally, he just blurted it out: "What am I missing, Coach? I'm here early, I stay late. I study the playbook every night."

Coach Turner crossed his arms, studying Bear with those assessing eyes. "You've got the work ethic, no doubt. But Greene's got the natural arm talent. Makes throws you can't."

The words stung because Bear knew they were true. Tyler could flick his wrist and send a perfect spiral 50 yards downfield. Bear had to put his whole body into the same throw.

"So I can't win the job," Bear said, dejection seeping into his voice.

"I didn't say that," Coach Turner replied sharply. "You asked what you're missing. I told you. Now it's on you to figure out how to make up the difference."

Coach turned to leave, then paused. "Wilson."

"Yes, Coach?"

"There's more to being a quarterback than a strong arm. Remember that."

Bear nodded, though he wasn't sure exactly what Coach meant. As he walked to the locker room, alone now on the empty field, the morning's encounter with Tony Brewer came back to him. The extra inch. The line he hadn't touched.

Was there a connection?

The rest of the school day passed in a blur. Bear was well-liked by teachers—a solid B+ student who never caused trouble—but today he couldn't focus on their lessons. His mind kept circling back to the problem of Tyler Greene and the seemingly insurmountable gap between them.

At lunch, he sat with Akeem Johnson, the team's star wide receiver and his best friend since elementary school.

"You look like someone stole your truck," Akeem said, unwrapping his sandwich.

Bear pushed his food around his plate. "Coach basically told me this morning that I can't compete with Tyler's arm talent."

"Well, yeah," Akeem said matter-of-factly. "Tyler's got a laser. Everyone knows that."

"Thanks for the support," Bear muttered.

Akeem rolled his eyes. "Come on, man. You know what I mean. Tyler's got the arm, but you've got other things. You're smarter with the ball. Better leader in the huddle. You never panic. You just need to focus on your strengths."

"My strengths aren't enough to win the starting job," Bear pointed out.

"Maybe not yet," Akeem conceded. "But you've got all summer. And hey, Tyler could always get hurt."

Bear frowned. "I don't want the job because someone gets injured. I want to earn it."

"Noble," Akeem said around a mouthful of chips. "Stupid, but noble."

After his last class, Bear stopped by his mother's classroom at the middle school next door. Ellen Wilson was grading papers when he knocked on the open door.

"Bear!" she said, looking up with a smile. "What brings you by?"

"Thought I'd say hi before heading home," he said, dropping into one of the student desks. "How are the essays?"

She made a face. "The usual. Half of them didn't read the book, a quarter of them read the SparkNotes, and a precious few actually have something original to say."

Bear chuckled. His mother's complaints about student writing were a constant refrain in their household.

"What's on your mind?" she asked, setting down her red pen. "You've got that look."

"What look?"

"The one you get when you're trying to solve a problem but can't quite figure it out."

Bear sighed. She could read him too well. "Coach says Tyler's still ahead of me because of his natural talent. His arm."

His mother nodded thoughtfully. "And that bothers you because you can't control your natural abilities."

"Exactly," Bear said. "I can work harder, study more, but I can't make my arm stronger than it is or my feet quicker than they are. Not enough to match Tyler, anyway."

"That's true," she agreed. "But natural talent isn't everything. I've taught thousands of students, Barrett. The naturally gifted ones often plateau because they've never had to work for their success. It's the ones who have to struggle, who have to find workarounds and develop systems, those are the ones who often go furthest."

Bear considered this. "So you're saying I might have an advantage because I have to work harder?"

BUT NATURAL TALENT ISN'T EVERYTHING.

"I'm saying don't count yourself out because someone else's path looks easier," she replied. "Your path might be tougher, but it could make you stronger in ways you don't yet see."

It wasn't a solution, but somehow it made Bear feel better. His mother had always had that effect on him—helping him see situations from a different angle, finding the silver lining without dismissing the clouds.

"Oh, I almost forgot," she added as he stood to leave. "A man stopped by my classroom during my planning period today. Tony Brewer. Said he met you the other day."

Bear paused. "Yeah. He caught me doing sprints after everyone left. Said something about the 'extra inch'—about touching the line even when you're tired."

His mother nodded. "Tony was exceptional—not just as a player but also as a student. One of those rare people who understood there was more to life than football."

Bear hadn't known that about Tony. In Jackson Creek lore, his legacy was almost entirely based on his exploits on the field, culminating in that state championship over two decades ago.

"He said he wanted to help me improve," Bear said. "Asked me to meet him at Arrington Hardware on Saturday morning."

"Are you going to go?"

Bear nodded. "Yeah. I mean, he's Tony Brewer. He's the best quarterback our school ever had. And I need all the help I can get if I want to compete with Tyler."

His mother studied him for a moment. "Just remember, Bear—there's more to being a quarterback than a strong arm."

It was the second time today someone had told him that. Bear wondered if maybe there was something important there that he was missing.

That evening, Bear was shooting baskets in his driveway, trying to clear his head. The rhythmic bounce of the ball and swoosh of the net provided a familiar comfort after a frustrating day. His father stepped outside, watching silently for a few minutes before walking over.

"Mind if I join?" Robert Wilson asked, catching a rebounding ball with practiced ease. Bear shrugged.

"Sure," he said.

His father took a shot from the edge of the driveway, sinking it cleanly. Despite being in his forties, Robert still had a smooth shooting form—a remnant from his own high school playing days.

"Heard spring ball wrapped up today," his father said casually, passing the ball back. "How'd it go?"

Bear caught the ball and held it, staring down at the worn leather. "Still number two on the depth chart."

"Behind Tyler Greene?"

"Yeah," Bear said with a sigh. "Coach says he's got more natural talent. A stronger arm."

His father nodded thoughtfully. "And what do you think?"

"He's right. Tyler's got the arm I don't."

Robert took the ball and dribbled a few times before taking another shot. "You know, I wasn't the most naturally talented player on my team either."

Bear looked up, somewhat surprised. His father rarely talked about his own athletic past.

"But you started, right? You have those trophies in the garage."

"Sure, but my sophomore year, I was riding the bench. Kid ahead of me was a natural athlete—faster, stronger, better jumper." His father retrieved the ball and passed it back. "But by senior year, I was starting, and he was watching from the sidelines most games."

"What changed?" Bear asked, genuinely curious.

"I figured out what game I was really playing," his father replied. "And it wasn't just basketball."

Bear frowned and said, "I don't understand."

"Most people don't," his father said with a knowing smile. "That's why they stay stuck."

They shot in comfortable silence for a few minutes, the familiar rhythm of their driveway sessions returning. Finally, his father spoke again.

"You know, I couldn't outjump the other guys, but I learned to read defenses better than anyone. Couldn't outrun them, but I could get to my spot before they knew where I was going. Sometimes the biggest advantage isn't physical at all."

Bear considered this, making a perfect swish through the net. "So you're saying I need to be smarter than Tyler, not try to throw harder than him?"

"I'm saying you need to understand your advantages instead of focusing on his," his father clarified. "By the way, you're still meeting Tony on Saturday, right?"

"Yes, sir," Bear confirmed. "Seven a.m. at Arrington Hardware."

"Good," his father said, nodding his approval. "Tony Brewer knows a thing or two about turning limitations into advantages. I think you'll learn a lot from him."

As they continued shooting, Bear felt something shift in his perspective. Maybe there was more than one way to win the quarterback competition after all.

What game was he really playing? And if the competition wasn't between him and Tyler Greene, then who was it with?

Saturday morning couldn't come soon enough.

CHAPTER 2
THE FIRST LESSON

The downtown of Jackson Creek consisted of about four blocks of storefronts surrounding the courthouse square. Arrington's Hardware had been a fixture on Main Street for as long as anyone could remember, owned and operated by three generations of Tony's family before being sold when his father retired. Bear pulled into a parking spot at 6:55 a.m., determined not to be late. The OPEN sign wasn't lit yet, but he could see movement inside. He approached the door, and Tony appeared, unlocking it to let him in.

"Right on time." Tony nodded and smiled. "First small victory of the day."

The store smelled of sawdust and metal, a combination Bear had always associated with his father's garage. Tony led him through the aisles to a door marked "Employees Only."

"I don't actually work here anymore," Tony explained as they entered a small back office, "but Bob still lets me use the space sometimes."

The office was simple—a desk, a few chairs, and a large whiteboard dominating the wall. On it, Tony had drawn what looked like a diagram. At the top was written "The Competitor's Choice," with two diverging paths below it. The left path was labeled "Drift Zone" and led to "Default Outcomes." The right path was labeled "Direction" and led to "Desired Outcomes." Between the paths was a slot labeled "Ego Gap."

Bear studied the board, trying to make sense of it. "What is this?"

"This," Tony said, tapping the board, "is the fundamental choice every person faces, every day. The choice between drifting toward what's easy or directing yourself toward what's excellent."

Tony gestured for Bear to take a seat, then picked up a marker. "Before we talk about football specifically, we need to understand the bigger picture. Because what I'm going to teach you isn't just about throwing a football. It's about life. It's about who you choose to become."

He pointed to the left side of the diagram. "Most people live here, in what I call the 'Drift Zone.' They follow the path of least resistance. They do what's comfortable, what everyone else is doing. They cut corners when they're tired. They skip the last rep when no one's watching."

Tony looked pointedly at Bear. "They don't touch the line."

Bear shifted uncomfortably, remembering their first meeting.

"The Drift Zone feels normal," Tony continued. "It doesn't feel like you're failing. It just feels like you're doing what everyone else does. But here's the thing—doing what everyone else does only gets you what everyone else gets. And most people aren't getting what they truly want."

He moved to the right side of the diagram. "This is where competitors live. Not athletes—competitors. People who make the conscious choice every day to direct themselves toward excellence, even when—especially when—it's hard."

"So what's the 'Ego Gap'?" Bear asked, pointing to the space between the paths.

"That," Tony said, "is the psychological barrier most people never cross. It's the space where your ego tries to protect itself through comfort, through excuses, through blaming circumstances or other people. Crossing it requires confronting uncomfortable truths about yourself."

As Tony explained the diagram, Bear noticed another figure passing by the store window—Tyler Greene, who paused briefly when he spotted them inside. Tyler's eyes met Bear's for a moment, then flicked to Tony with what seemed like recognition before he continued walking.

"Do you know Tyler?" Bear asked, curious about the brief exchange.

Tony nodded casually. "I know most of the players in town. Coach Turner and I talk football sometimes."

He returned to the whiteboard, his focus completely on Bear now. "But today isn't about Tyler. It's about you understanding the fundamental choice that shapes everything else."

He put down the marker and sat across from Bear. "Let me ask you something—why do you want to be the starting quarterback?"

The question seemed obvious, but Bear sensed there was more to it. "Because I've worked for it. I want to lead the team. I want to prove I can do it."

"And what happens if you don't get it? If Tyler stays the starter all season?"

Bear hesitated. "I guess . . . I'd be disappointed. Frustrated."

"Would you feel like a failure?"

The question hit deeper than Bear expected. "Maybe. Yeah, probably."

Tony nodded. "That's the ego talking. It says that your worth, your identity, is tied to outcomes—to being the starter, to beating Tyler. And as long as that's true, you'll never cross the Ego Gap, because your fear of failure will keep you playing it safe."

Bear frowned. "Playing it safe? I work harder than anyone on the team."

"Working hard isn't the same as taking risks," Tony replied. "The biggest risk isn't physical—it's psychological. It's being willing to define success differently than most people do."

He stood and walked back to the whiteboard, drawing a horizontal line on either side of the Ego Gap.

"This is what I call 'The Competitor's Choice.' It's the daily decision to compete not against others but against the limita-

THE BIGGEST RISK ISN'T PHYSICAL—IT'S PSYCHOLOGICAL. IT'S BEING WILLING TO DEFINE SUCCESS DIFFERENTLY THAN MOST PEOPLE DO.

tions you place on yourself. It's choosing direction over drift, every single day."

Tony tapped the board where the words "Default Outcomes" were written. "Think about what happens if you continue on your current path. Working hard, yes, but still defining success as 'beating Tyler.' What's the default outcome?"

Bear thought about it. "Either I beat him out, or I don't. I either succeed or fail."

"Exactly. And you've set it up so there's only one way to win, and it depends on someone else. That's a losing strategy."

He moved his marker to "Desired Outcomes" on the right side. "But what if you defined success differently? What if winning wasn't about beating Tyler, but about becoming the absolute best version of Bear Wilson possible? What would that look like?"

The question landed differently than Bear expected. He'd been so focused on comparing himself to Tyler that he hadn't really considered what his own excellence might look like independent of anyone else.

"I'm not sure," he admitted.

"That's where we start," Tony said with a nod. "Getting clear on what game you're really playing. And I'll tell you right now—it's not the game most people think it is."

Tony moved to another portion of the whiteboard, where letters were written vertically: COMPETE.

"This is the framework I've developed over the years. It's how you cross the Ego Gap and move from drift to direction. It's how you make The Competitor's Choice, day after day."

Bear leaned forward, intrigued despite his initial skepticism.

"'C' stands for *Clarify*," Tony explained. "Before you can win any game, you have to know exactly what game you're playing."

"Football," Bear said automatically. "Quarterback."

Tony shook his head. "That's the surface game. The deeper game is about who you're becoming through the process. And before you can clarify that, you need to get honest about who you're really competing with."

"Tyler Greene," Bear said, though with less certainty now.

"Is it?" Tony challenged. "Let me ask you this—that day on the field, when you didn't touch the line, who were you competing with then?"

Bear was quiet, the realization dawning on him. "Myself, I guess. My own laziness. My willingness to accept 'good enough.'"

"Exactly," Tony said, his voice softening. "The most important competition—the one that determines whether you reach your potential—is the one between who you are today and who you could become tomorrow."

He sat on the edge of the desk. "When you were running those sprints by yourself that day I first met you, and you didn't touch the line, who were you cheating?"

Bear looked down. "Myself."

"Not Tyler Greene. Not Coach Turner. *Yourself.* And that's the first lesson of touching the line—understanding that your primary competition is against your own potential, your own standards, your own discipline."

Bear nodded, but inside, he was conflicted. The idea of competing against himself, of focusing on the process rather than the outcome, was foreign to him. He'd always measured success by wins and losses, by being better than the guy next to him. Could he really shift his mindset to see the value in these small, invisible choices? What if touching the line didn't actually make a difference in his game?

Tony walked back to The Competitor's Choice diagram. "Most people drift through life comparing themselves to others. It's a race to the middle, where you define success as being slightly better than the next guy. But competitors—*true* competitors—are playing a different game entirely.

"They compete not just with others but against *themselves*."

The distinction clicked something into place for Bear. "So you're saying I shouldn't be trying to beat Tyler? That doesn't make sense. Only one of us can start."

"I'm saying that your focus on beating Tyler is actually limiting you," Tony explained. "When your goal is just to be better than someone else, you'll never discover your own unique potential. You'll always be playing their game, on their terms."

He moved back to the COMPETE framework. "So the first question is: What game are you playing, Bear? What's the real competition here?"

Bear thought for a long moment. "I'm competing against . . . the part of me that wants to take shortcuts. The part that's willing to settle for less than my best."

"Good start," Tony said, nodding. "But there's more to it. Why does this competition matter to you? What's at stake?"

"Being the starting quarterback," Bear said, but seeing Tony's expression, he

reconsidered. "No, it's more than that. It's about proving to myself that I can achieve something difficult, something that doesn't come naturally to me."

"Now we're getting somewhere!" Tony exclaimed. "When you clarify what game you're really playing and why it matters deeply to you, everything else starts to fall into place."

He sat down across from Bear. "Most people never clearly define what game they're playing, so they end up playing the wrong game—trying to win at things that don't actually matter to them."

"Like what?" Bear asked.

"Like focusing on beating Tyler Greene instead of becoming the best possible version of yourself," Tony explained. "If your goal is just to be better than Tyler, what happens if he transfers schools? Have you won? Or what if he improves faster than you can keep up with? Have you lost?"

Bear had never thought of it that way before.

"But if your competition is against your own potential," Tony continued, "then you can win regardless of what Tyler does. Your success isn't dependent on someone else's failure."

"But only one of us can be the starter," Bear pointed out, still struggling with this concept.

"True," Tony acknowledged. "That's the external outcome. But there's also an internal outcome—who you become through the process. And that's actually more valuable in the long run."

Bear wasn't entirely convinced. He still wanted to be the starter, not just someone who developed good character while sitting on the bench.

Tony seemed to read his mind. "I'm not saying the starting position doesn't matter. It does. But how you pursue it matters more than whether you achieve it."

He stood up and paced the small office. "Think about it this way—what if you cut corners, cheat reps, take shortcuts, and somehow still win the starting job? You might have the position, but you'd know deep down that you didn't earn it. That would eat at you, undermine your confidence in crucial moments."

"But what if I do everything right and still don't win the job?" Bear asked, voicing his deepest fear.

"Then you've still won the more important game," Tony said simply. "You've developed discipline and character that will serve you long after football is over. And you've put yourself in position to succeed in the future, whether that's later this season, next year, or in some completely different arena."

He pointed back to The Competitor's Choice diagram. "Most people stay in the Drift Zone because they're afraid to cross the Ego Gap. They're afraid of failure, of looking bad, of discovering that their best might not be good enough. So they protect their ego with excuses, with blame, with shortcuts."

"But competitors," Tony continued, his voice intensifying, "they make a different choice. They're willing to risk their ego for their potential. They understand that temporary failures are just information—feedback that helps them grow. They know that touching the line when it's hardest is exactly what builds the strength to cross the Ego Gap."

Bear was quiet, absorbing this new perspective. It was challenging everything he'd ever thought about competition, about success, about what it meant to win.

"Let me tell you something about water and ice," Tony said, changing direction. "Do you know the difference between them, temperature-wise?"

Bear raised an eyebrow at the seemingly random question. "Uh, one degree? Water freezes at thirty-two degrees Fahrenheit."

"Exactly. Just one degree," Tony confirmed. "At thirty-three degrees, water flows freely. At thirty-two degrees, it becomes solid. One more degree colder, and it's strong enough to support weight. One degree of difference completely transforms its nature and capabilities."

Tony leaned in toward Bear to emphasize his next point. "Most people live their entire lives at thirty-three degrees—

just one degree away from transformation. They're good but never great. They come close but never truly arrive.

"They *almost* touch the line."

Bear was beginning to see the connection. "So you're saying that extra inch—touching the line—is like dropping that one degree?"

"Precisely," Tony said, clearly pleased that Bear was catching on. "It's the small choices, consistently made, that create the one-degree difference between water and ice . . . between potential and accomplishment . . . between good and great."

He glanced at his watch. "That's enough for today. I want you to think about what we've discussed. Really think about it. Start a journal. Each night, write down three things: what game you played that day, who or what you competed against, and why it mattered."

"A journal?" Bear repeated skeptically. "That's not really my thing."

"Wasn't mine either," Tony admitted. "And we'll get into it more later, but the 'T' in COMPETE is *Take Time*: Remember to Reflect, Review, and Rest. It's just as crucial to review our day for lessons learned as it is to watch tape after practices and Friday-night games. Most people are too busy jumping into the next day to reflect on what they did well and where they can improve from today forward.

"But trust me on this. Writing it down makes it real. Makes you accountable to yourself. And it helps you track whether you're drifting or directing yourself each day."

As Bear stood to leave, Tony added, "Next time, we'll talk about the 'O' in COMPETE—*Observe*: Know the Rules to Win the Game." He tapped The Competitor's Choice diagram once more. "But remember, all of this comes back to the fundamental choice—drift or direction. Default or desired. Every day, we either accept what comes or create what could be."

Bear nodded, his mind spinning with new ideas and challenges. He'd come here expecting football drills—mechanics, footwork, throwing techniques. Instead, he'd gotten a philosophy lesson that seemed both strangely disconnected from and deeply relevant to his quarterback competition.

"See you next Saturday?" Tony asked.

"Yes, sir," Bear confirmed. "Same time?"

"Same time. But next session will be at the field. Principles need practice to become real."

Tony walked him to the door. "And Bear? Start making The Competitor's Choice today. In small ways. Touch the line even when no one's watching. That's how you begin crossing the Ego Gap."

As Bear drove home, The Competitor's Choice diagram kept replaying in his mind: Drift versus Direction. Default Outcomes versus Desired Outcomes. The Ego Gap that separated them.

Had he been drifting all this time, even while working hard? Was his focus on beating Tyler actually holding him back from discovering his own potential?

TOUCH THE LINE EVEN WHEN NO ONE'S WATCHING.

And most importantly—was he brave enough to cross the Ego Gap? To define success not by comparison to others but by competition with himself?

Bear grabbed his backpack from beside the front door, intending to review some playbook concepts before bed. Inside was also his summer reading assignment for Advanced English—a class his mother had encouraged him to take despite his reservations.

Math and history had always come easily to him—concrete facts, clear rules, stories with beginnings and endings. He maintained solid B+ grades in those without much strain. But English literature, with its symbols and subjective interpretations, and science, with its abstract concepts and formulas . . . those were different challenges entirely. The notebook Tony had asked him to keep would be yet another form of writing to manage.

Bear set the English assignment aside for tomorrow. Tonight, he'd focus on processing what Tony had shared. If he could master that framework, maybe it would help him tackle other challenges too—on and off the field.

Bear sat at his desk with his blank notebook open in front of him. He felt slightly ridiculous, but Tony's words kept echoing in his head: Writing it down makes it real.

Finally, he began:

Today's Game: Learning what competition really means

My Competition: The part of me that wants to take the easy way out

Why It Matters: Because I want to earn my success, not just be given it or luck into it

He stared at the words for a while, then added:

The Competitor's Choice: Today I realized I might be playing the wrong game. I've been so focused on beating Tyler Greene that I haven't considered what it would mean to be the best version of myself, regardless of anyone else.

What if the competition isn't really between me and Tyler? What if it's between who I am now and who I could become?

Bear closed the notebook, not entirely convinced but feeling like maybe, just maybe, he was starting to understand what Tony was trying to teach him. The path forward wasn't clear yet, but for the first time in months, he felt something shifting—a new perspective taking root.

One degree of difference. Water to ice. Good to great.

The question was: Could he make that transformation? Could he cross the Ego Gap and discover what waited on the other side?

CHAPTER 3

TOUCHING THE LINE

The June sun was climbing higher in the Texas sky with each passing day, bringing with it the trademark heat that would soon make outdoor training brutal. The Saturday morning was still bearable as Bear arrived at the field fifteen minutes early. The grass was wet with dew, the rising sun casting long shadows across the turf. He used the time to stretch and warm up, his mind clearer than it had been in weeks.

When Tony arrived, carrying a bag of footballs and what looked like a stack of index cards, he nodded approvingly at Bear's early arrival.

"Making The Competitor's Choice already," he observed. "Good."

"Just didn't want to be late," Bear replied, though he felt a small surge of pride at the acknowledgment.

"Choices become habits, habits become character," Tony reminded him, setting down his equipment. "But before we start, tell me—did you write in your journal last night?"

"I did," Bear admitted, feeling slightly self-conscious.

"And did you think about what we discussed? About the real competition?"

Bear nodded. "I think so. It's not really about beating Tyler. It's about becoming the best version of myself."

Tony smiled, displaying genuine approval in his expression. "You're catching on quick. Most guys your age would have pushed back harder against that idea."

Bear shrugged. "My dad said something similar when I told him about our conversation. About focusing on what you can control instead of comparing yourself to others."

"Smart man, your father," Tony said. "Now, let's move to the second letter in our framework. We covered 'C' for *Clarify* yesterday. Today it's 'O' for *Observe*: Know the Rules to Win the Game."

Bear looked confused. "I know the rules of football."

"Not those rules," Tony clarified. "The rules of excellence. The nonnegotiables of becoming great at anything."

He handed Bear the stack of index cards. Each one had a simple statement written on it: *Control the controllables. Process over outcome. Measure what matters. Small choices compound.*

Bear flipped to the top card: *Can't see, Can't miss,* it read.

"What does that mean?" Bear asked.

"The things others don't see you choose are what compound to create the results others can't miss you earning," Tony explained.

"Most people only see the touchdown pass on Friday night. They don't see the extra throwing sessions, the film study, the proper nutrition, the good sleep habits. Those invisible choices compound over time into visible results that seem like they came out of nowhere."

He gestured to the cards in Bear's hand. "These are some of the rules of excellence. Let's focus on the first one today: Every rep counts."

Bear studied the cards, running his thumb along the edges. "So these are the rules for excellence?"

"The *foundations*," Tony corrected. "And they apply to everything—football, academics, relationships, life." He took a water bottle from his bag, unscrewed the cap, and took a drink before continuing.

"Let me share something about why these small choices matter so much. Remember what I told you about water and ice—that one-degree difference?"

Bear nodded. "At thirty-three degrees, water flows freely. At thirty-two degrees, it becomes solid."

"Exactly," Tony said. "Most people dismiss that one degree because they don't notice much difference when they change the temperature in their house from seventy-three to seventy-four. But that single degree, that one small choice, that slight extra effort can change everything."

He pointed to the end zone. "It's the difference between touching the line and coming close. Between excellence and mediocrity. Between being good and being great."

The concept was starting to click for Bear. "So the small things that seem insignificant—"

"Are actually the difference-makers," Tony said, finishing Bear's thought. "Tyler Greene might have more natural arm talent than you. You can't control that. But you can control whether you touch the line every time. Whether you complete every rep with purpose. Whether you maintain your mechanics when you're tired."

He picked up a football. "Show me your throwing motion."

Bear went through his motion without the ball, the same way he'd practiced thousands of times.

Tony shook his head. "Do it again, but this time, imagine it's fourth down, state championship on the line."

Bear repeated the motion, concentrating harder, imagining the pressure. "Better," Tony said. "Now, what was different?"

Bear thought about it. "I was more focused the second time."

"Exactly," Tony said. "And that's the problem with how most people practice. They go through the motions without purpose. They don't treat every rep like it matters. They're content to stay at thirty-three degrees when thirty-two transforms everything."

He handed Bear a football. "For the next hour, we're going to work on your mechanics. But here's the rule: every single throw has to be made with championship-level focus. If I see you going through the motions even once, we start over."

As they began their drills, Bear noticed a small group of middle schoolers watching from beyond the fence line. They were clearly football players, huddled together and pointing occasionally as Bear worked through his throwing motion. One boy in particular—lanky with an athletic build despite his youth—watched with unusual intensity.

"Audience today," Bear commented as he completed a set of 5-step drops.

Tony glanced over his shoulder. "Rising eighth graders. Summer youth program. That focused one in front is Max Jenkins. Coach says he's got a cannon for an arm, might be special when he gets to high school."

Bear nodded but didn't think much more about it. He had his own development to worry about. Tony handed him another football, and they continued working.

The next hour was one of the most mentally exhausting of Bear's life. Tony made him focus on the tiniest details of his throwing motion—foot placement, hip rotation, follow-through. Every time Bear's concentration slipped, Tony would call him on it, making him start the drill over.

"This is the difference," Tony explained as they took a water break. "Tyler Greene might have more natural talent, but talent without discipline is like a car with no driver. It might look good in the driveway, but it won't take you anywhere."

Bear nodded, beginning to understand. "So touching the line is about doing every rep with purpose."

IT'S ABOUT UNDERSTANDING THAT EXCELLENCE ISN'T AN EVENT—IT'S A HABIT.

"Exactly," Tony confirmed. "It's about respecting the process enough to give it your complete attention. It's about understanding that excellence isn't an event—it's a habit."

Tony picked up another football, tossing it lightly between his hands. "Let me ask you something, Bear. Have you ever heard the story of Sisyphus?"

Bear shook his head. "Sounds familiar, but I don't think so."

"Sisyphus was a figure in Greek mythology," Tony explained, sitting down on a nearby bench and gesturing for Bear to join him. "The gods punished him by forcing him to roll a massive boulder up a steep hill, only to watch it roll back down every time he neared the top. Then he'd have to start all over again. Forever."

Bear frowned. "That sounds . . . terrible."

"Most people think so," Tony agreed. "They see it as the ultimate futile task—endless effort with no achievement, no completion. Just the same struggle, day after day."

"Isn't it, though?" Bear asked.

Tony smiled thoughtfully. "That's the conventional view. But there's another way to look at it. A philosopher named Camus suggested something different—that we should imagine Sisyphus happy."1

"Happy?" Bear looked incredulous. "Pushing a rock uphill forever with nothing to show for it?"

"Think about it this way," Tony said. "What if Sisyphus found meaning not in getting the rock to stay at the top, but in the process itself? What if he took pride in how he pushed the rock each time—the technique he developed, the strength he built, the resilience he showed?"

Bear considered this. "So . . . it's about finding value in the process rather than just the outcome?"

"Exactly," Tony said, nodding. "Most people are so focused on the destination that they miss the journey. They only measure success by endpoints—touchdowns, championships, grades, promotions. But true competitors understand that excellence lives in the process."

"Like touching the line," Bear said slowly, the connection becoming clear.

"Precisely. When you touch the line on every sprint, complete every rep with full focus, study the playbook with total concentration—you're finding meaning in the process itself. You're becoming Sisyphus, who rolls his boulder with purpose and pride, regardless of whether it stays at the top."

Tony stood up, tossing the football to Bear. "Everyone faces their own boulder—daily challenges that seem repetitive, arduous tasks that might not have immediate payoff. Most people resent the boulder. They push halfheartedly, looking for shortcuts, counting the minutes until they can stop pushing."

"But competitors," he continued, "Competitors embrace the boulder. They see each push as an opportunity to get stronger, to refine their technique, to build character that others lack. They understand that how you push your boulder defines who you become, regardless of where the boulder ends up."

Bear nodded, a new understanding dawning. "So it's not just about touching the line to get better at football. It's about who I become through the process of going that extra inch."

"Now you're getting it," Tony said approvingly. "The outcome—whether you become the starter or not—is important.

But it's secondary to who you become through the process. That's the real victory."

"And when the boulder rolls back down?" Bear asked.

"You smile," Tony said simply. "Because you know something others don't—that the pushing itself has value. That excellence isn't a destination you reach once; it's a daily choice to engage fully with whatever boulder you're pushing."

Bear rolled the football between his hands, processing this new perspective. "So even if I do everything right and still don't win the starting job—"

"Then you've still won the more important game," Tony said, finishing Bear's thought. "You've developed discipline and character that will serve you long after football is over."

Tony's expression grew more serious. "Let me tell you a story from when I was about your age. It wasn't about football, but the lesson still applies."

Bear leaned in, curious.

"I was a freshman in high school, during off-season training. We were in the weight room doing a lower body lifting session. My partner and I were trading sets of different exercises, and neither of us wanted to do all three sets of ten reps when it came time for back squats."

Bear could already see where this was going.

"So we made a deal to quietly do just two sets instead of three. We'd take our time, rotate slower than normal, and stay busy enough that no one would notice." Tony shook his head at the memory. "When the whistle blew to change stations, we racked the weights and started heading to the next station."

"Did you get caught?" Bear asked.

Tony nodded. "Coach Long blew a second whistle, had everyone take a knee, and asked my partner and me if we'd done all three sets. He knew the truth, and he was giving us the chance to either come clean or dig our graves deeper."

"What did you do?"

"We confessed. And man, did we pay for it." Tony laughed as he remembered the pain that followed. "The entire team had to do pushups because of our laziness. Then my partner and I got sent outside to run hill sprints—felt like a hundred of them."

Bear winced. "That's rough."

"It was fair," Tony countered. "But what stuck with me was what Coach Long said afterward. He told me, 'If you're not going to be accountable to yourself to do your best when no one is watching, then how are your teammates in the locker room going to rely on you? If you can't show up with one hundred percent effort on things you don't necessarily want to do, do you think you can lead others to do so?

"You have to be a leader who does what's right and what's *needed*, regardless of whether a coach is watching or you want to be doing it.'"

Bear was quiet, absorbing the story.

"That day changed me," Tony continued. "I realized that cutting corners—even when no one sees it—has a cost. It erodes your character. It makes you the kind of person who takes shortcuts. And, eventually, that catches up to you."

He pointed to his water bottle. "It's that one degree. The difference between solid and liquid. Between potential and achievement. I chose to drop the temperature that day, to hold myself to a standard that would transform me, not just my performance."

"Did you ever cheat reps again?" Bear asked.

Tony smiled. "Never. Not once. Because I understood it wasn't about the reps—it was about who I was becoming."

"You know," Tony said, "Coach Turner told me he sees something similar in you."

Bear looked up, surprised. "He talks to you about me?"

"We discuss the team sometimes. He's concerned about all his players," Tony replied carefully. "He mentioned how you've been putting in the extra work. Said you remind him of me at your age—driven, dedicated, just needing the right guidance to channel it."

Bear felt a strange mix of pride and pressure. Coach Turner had noticed his effort after all, but just hadn't said anything directly to him.

"Coach isn't big on compliments," Tony added with a knowing smile. "He believes praise should be earned through consistent excellence, not occasional effort. But trust me—he sees what you're doing."

He gestured to the field. "You know why I had you meet me here today instead of at the hardware store?"

Bear shook his head.

"Because principles without practice are just good intentions. You need to feel what it's like to touch the line, not just understand the concept."

Tony took the ball back from Bear. "Now, let's put this philosophy into practice. I want you to throw ten out-routes to that cone. But here's the twist—after each throw, I want you to write down one thing you noticed about your technique."

"Write it down?" Bear asked. "Like in the journal?"

"Similar idea," Tony said. "Tracking what you observe creates awareness. Awareness leads to improvement."

For the next fifteen minutes, Bear threw and made notes after each throw. By the tenth throw, he was noticing details about his mechanics that he'd never paid attention to before.

"Now, look at your notes," Tony instructed. "What patterns do you see?"

Bear reviewed what he'd written: "I'm not following through enough on my longer throws. And I'm rushing when I feel tired."

"Good observations," Tony said. "Now you know what to focus on tomorrow. That's how improvement works—observe, adjust, repeat."

As they gathered the equipment, Tony said, "For your journal tonight, I want you to add something. Write down what metrics you're going to track to measure your improvement."

"Metrics?" Bear asked.

"The things that matter," Tony explained. "Completion percentage, sure. But also things like: How many perfect reps did I do today? How many times did I touch the line when I was tired? How many times did I choose the harder right over the easier wrong?"

Bear nodded, beginning to see how all of this connected. "So the extra inch is also about measuring the right things."

"You're catching on," Tony said, his approval evident in his voice. "Remember, what gets measured gets improved."

He took one last look at the field before they left. "One more thing to remember, Bear. Most people live their entire lives at thirty-three degrees—just one degree away from transfor-

ONE DEGREE. ONE CHOICE. ONE EXTRA INCH OF EFFORT TO TOUCH THE LINE. THAT'S ALL IT TAKES TO CHANGE EVERYTHING.

mation. They're good, but never great. They come close, but never truly arrive. They convince themselves that one degree doesn't matter."

"But it does," Bear said, understanding now.

"More than most people ever realize," Tony affirmed. "One degree. One choice. One extra inch of effort to touch the line. That's all it takes to change everything."

"I think I'm starting to get it," Bear said. "But can I really make up for Tyler's natural talent just by paying attention to these small details?"

Tony considered the question. "You're still thinking about it the wrong way. The goal isn't to be Tyler. The goal is to be the best possible version of you."

He picked up a football and tossed it to Bear. "Let me ask you something. Who's the better quarterback: the one who can throw the ball seventy yards but completes forty percent of his passes, or the one who can only throw it fifty yards but completes sixty-five percent?"

Bear caught the ball easily. "The second one, obviously."

"Exactly. So stop focusing on what you can't do—throw as far as Tyler—and start focusing on what you can do: make smart decisions, improve your accuracy, lead your teammates effectively. If you're busy trying to be Tyler, you'll never discover your own strengths. And those strengths might be exactly what this team needs."

The concept was liberating. Bear realized he had spent so much time trying to match Tyler's natural abilities that he'd neglected to develop his own unique talents.

"It's like that old saying," Tony continued. "The fox who tries to climb a tree will always be disappointed. But the fox who masters the ground can outmaneuver anyone."

Bear nodded, a new sense of possibility emerging. "So instead of trying to be a different version of Tyler, I need to be a better version of myself."

"Now you're getting it," Tony said, clapping him on the shoulder. "And that starts with touching the line—being disciplined in the small things, treating every rep as if it matters, understanding that excellence is built one degree at a time."

As Bear walked to his car, his legs heavy from the workout with Tony, he spotted a group of varsity players gathering at the field entrance. Tyler was among them, laughing as he tossed a football effortlessly to a teammate.

"Wilson! Done with your extra session?" Tyler called out, his tone casual but with an undercurrent Bear couldn't quite place.

"Yeah," Bear replied, suddenly aware of how sweaty and exhausted he must look compared to the fresh, relaxed appearance of his teammates.

"Man, Bear's always doing extra work," someone commented. "You trying to make us all look bad?"

There was laughter, not mean-spirited but not entirely friendly either. Bear felt a strange mix of pride, unease, and self-consciousness.

"Just working on some things," he said simply.

Tyler studied him for a moment. "Well, don't overdo it. We've got team conditioning tomorrow. Coach isn't gonna go easy just because you're tired."

As Bear drove home, those words echoed in his mind. Was he doing too much? Would the extra work actually help him compete with Tyler's natural talent, or was he just exhausting himself for nothing?

He thought about Tony's water and ice analogy. The one-degree difference. If he was right, then these extra sessions, these moments of pushing when others rested—that was the degree that would transform him.

But doubt crept in too. What if Tony was wrong? What if some people were just meant to be water, and others ice? What if all this talk about "touching the line" was just a way to make average players feel better about never being great?

Bear shook his head, forcing those thoughts away. He'd chosen his path. He would touch the line, day after day, and see where it led him.

"One degree," he whispered to himself as he pulled into his driveway. "Water to ice. Good to great."

The question was: Could he make that transformation? Or would all this extra work just leave him more tired than everyone else, with nothing to show for it?

He thought of all the small corners he'd cut over the years—the extra reps he'd skipped when he was tired, the study sessions he'd shortened when he got bored, the times he'd relied on natural ability instead of pushing for excellence. How many opportunities for transformation had he missed?

At home, he found his father in the garage, organizing tools with his usual meticulous care.

"Hey, Dad," Bear called, setting down his gear. "Need some help?"

Robert Wilson glanced up with a smile. "Sure. I'm reorganizing the toolbox. Everything has its place."

Bear joined him, handing tools as his father called for them. "Tony told me about the difference between water and ice today," he said after a while. "How one degree changes everything."

His father nodded thoughtfully. "He's right. I see it in business all the time. The difference between a good year and a great year isn't usually some massive change. It's a hundred small improvements that compound."

That evening, Bear sat at his desk, journal open, thinking about what he'd learned. He wrote:

Today's Game: Learning to focus on every rep

Who I'm Competing With: The lazy part of me

Why It Matters: Because you can't fake it in real games

I'm starting to get what Tony means about water freezing at thirty-two degrees. When I'm tired, it's so tempting to go through the motions. But today I felt the difference when I really focused on each throw. My completion percentage was way higher.

The Sisyphus story is weird, but it makes me think. What if practice isn't just something to get through? What if the rock pushing is the point?

One degree. That's it. Just one degree between water and ice. Between good and great. I need to drop my temperature just one more degree.

As June gave way to July, Bear found himself applying Tony's principles not just to football training, but to every aspect of his life. The discipline of touching the line—of going that extra inch when it would be easier to cut corners—was becoming a habit, a mindset that transferred beyond the practice field.

With the blistering heat of early July settling over Jackson Creek, Bear was about to discover that his greatest challenge might not be on the football field at all.

CHAPTER 4

THE CHEATED REP

The July sun beat down mercilessly on the Jackson Creek practice facilities, turning the metal bleachers into furnaces and the turf into a heat-radiating griddle. Summer conditioning was in full swing, with players reporting to the field house four days a week for Coach Turner's notorious workout regimen.

Bear had been up since dawn, reviewing the offensive playbook Tony had helped him break down during their Saturday session. The concepts of "touching the line" and the "one-degree difference" had taken root in his thinking, but something still nagged at him—a question of whether these principles would actually make a difference when it mattered.

In the field house, he overheard a sophomore receiver complaining to a teammate as they filled their water bottles. "Man, I heard Turner's running hill sprints today. Ten rounds."

"Seriously? In this heat?" his friend groaned. "Someone's gonna pass out."

Bear felt his stomach tighten. Hill sprints were notorious—40 yards of quad-burning punishment up the steep incline behind the end zone—a challenge that had broken many players' spirits over the years. This would be his first real test of Tony's principles under genuine team pressure.

As he taped his ankles in preparation, Bear spotted Akeem entering the field house, already sweating from his warm-up jog.

"Ready for 'Murder Hill' this afternoon?" Bear asked.

Akeem rolled his eyes. "As ready as anyone can be for that torture. Coach is in some kind of mood this week."

"Yeah," Bear agreed, then hesitated before adding, "You know, I've been thinking about something Tony Brewer told me last Saturday—about how excellence is built in those moments when it would be easier to cut corners."

"That's great for Tony Brewer," Akeem said with a hint of skepticism. "State champion, college star—some guys just have that extra gear, you know? The rest of us are just trying to survive Coach's conditioning without puking."

Bear wanted to explain that wasn't Tony's point—that the "extra gear" wasn't something you were born with but something you built through small choices—but Coach Turner's whistle cut through the air, calling everyone to the field.

As they jogged out into the blistering heat, Bear wondered if maybe Akeem was right. Maybe some people were just born with that capacity for excellence, and others weren't. Maybe Tyler was just naturally gifted in ways Bear could never match, no matter how many lines he touched.

But then he remembered Tony's certainty, the conviction in his voice when he talked about the one-degree difference. And then he made a decision: Today's hill sprints would be his testing ground. He would complete every rep, touch every line, and see if it actually made a difference. Not just in his conditioning but in his mindset.

Because if Tony was right, the real competition wasn't against Tyler or anyone else on the team. It was against that voice inside that said cutting corners just this once wouldn't matter.

As the team gathered at the base of the hill, Bear spotted Tyler Greene in the group. Unlike most of the others who looked apprehensive about the coming workout, Tyler appeared almost relaxed, confident. Something about his demeanor caught Bear's attention—a subtle but noticeable change from his usual casualness toward conditioning.

Coach Turner's voice boomed across the field. "Listen up! Ten stations, one minute at each, then sprint up the hill behind the end zone and back. Three rounds. No breaks between stations."

The team groaned collectively, but Bear kept his expression neutral. This was his opportunity to choose direction over drift, to separate himself through the small choices others might miss.

"Greene, Wilson," Coach called out. "You two demonstrate the stations for the team."

As Bear moved forward alongside Tyler, he couldn't help but notice something different in Tyler's approach too—a focus, an intentionality that hadn't been there before. Had Tony been talking to him as well?

But there wasn't time to dwell on it. The challenge was about to begin, and Bear was determined to touch every line, complete every rep, and prove to himself that the extra-inch difference was more than just talk.

Bear and Tyler moved through each station as Coach explained the exercises—burpees, mountain climbers, jump squats, and more. By the time they finished demonstrating, Bear was already feeling the burn in his muscles. The real challenge was still to come.

"All right, break into groups of five," Coach instructed. "First group on stations, the rest of you on the hill."

Bear ended up in a group with Akeem and three other juniors. They tackled the first round of stations with energy, but by the time they hit the hill, everyone was feeling it. Bear pushed himself up the incline, legs burning, lungs screaming for oxygen. At the top, he turned and headed back down, making sure to touch the line at the bottom before rejoining his group for the second round of stations.

By the third round, exhaustion had set in. Bear was at the jump squat station, counting out the reps in his head, when he noticed Akeem at the burpee station next to him. Akeem was counting out loud, but Bear realized something wasn't right. The count didn't match the reps.

"Twenty-eight, twenty-nine, thirty," Akeem counted, but he'd only done about twenty-five burpees.

Bear said nothing, focusing on his own station. When the whistle blew, they rotated, and Bear moved to the burpee station.

"Thirty burpees," Coach called out as the timer started.

Bear began the grueling exercise—down to a push-up position, push-up, jump to standing, jump with hands overhead, back down. He counted each one carefully, fighting through the burn in his muscles.

By twenty-five, his arms were shaking. He glanced around. No one was watching him directly. Coach Turner was focused on another group. He could easily skip the last five, say he'd done thirty, and no one would know.

Except he would know.

The Competitor's Choice materialized in his mind—drift or direction? Default or desired? In this moment of fatigue, when every fiber of his body wanted to take the easy path, the true test revealed itself.

Every rep counts.

With a surge of determination, Bear pushed through the final five burpees, completing all thirty just as the whistle blew again.

As they moved to the hill for the final time, Bear noticed that Tyler, in another group, seemed to be cruising through the workout, barely breaking a sweat. But when Tyler reached the top of the hill, he turned and came back down without quite touching the line at the bottom before rejoining his group.

Bear felt a flash of frustration. Here he was, pushing himself to do every rep honestly, touch every line, while the starting quarterback was cutting corners. And no one seemed to notice or care.

The rest of the workout passed in a blur of sweat and exertion. By the time they finished, Bear's legs felt like jelly, and his T-shirt was soaked through. The team gathered around the water coolers, everyone chugging water and trying to recover.

"Good work today, men," Coach Turner called out. "That's the kind of effort that wins championships. Hit the showers."

As the team dispersed, Bear found himself walking alongside Akeem, who was still breathing hard.

"Man, those burpees are killers," Akeem said.

Bear hesitated, his mind racing. He knew what Tony would say—touching the line mattered, even when no one was watching. But calling out a teammate, especially someone as respected as Akeem, was risky. What if it backfired? What if it made things worse? The weight of the decision pressed down on him, but he knew he couldn't just let it go.

"I noticed you skipped a few," he said.

Akeem gave him a surprised look. "What?"

"On the burpees. You counted to thirty but only did about twenty-five."

Akeem's expression shifted from surprise to defensiveness. "Everyone does that, Bear. It's just a few reps. No big deal."

"Is it, though?" Bear asked. "I mean, if we're all pushing to get better, isn't cheating reps kind of . . . cheating ourselves?"

Akeem rolled his eyes. "Look at you, Mr. Perfect. It's summer conditioning, not the state championship. Save the intensity for when it matters."

"But that's the thing," Bear insisted, remembering Tony's words. "It does matter. The habits we build now show up when it counts. Those invisible choices become visible results."

"Whatever, man," Akeem said, clearly uncomfortable with the conversation. "I gotta hit the showers."

As Akeem walked away, Bear felt a pang of regret. Had he overstepped? Was he being self-righteous? Or was he simply holding himself and his teammates to the standard they all deserved?

Before he could ponder it further, Coach Turner called out, "Wilson, Greene—a word." Bear exchanged a glance with Tyler as they approached the coach.

"Good work today, both of you," Coach said. "But I noticed something." He looked directly at Tyler. "Greene, you didn't touch the line on your last hill sprint."

Tyler's confident expression faltered slightly. "Sorry, Coach. I was tired."

"We're all tired," Coach replied evenly. "That's the point of conditioning." He turned to Bear. "Wilson, I saw you complete every rep, touch every line, even when you thought no one was watching. That's the kind of discipline that makes a difference."

Bear was stunned. Coach had been watching more closely than he'd realized.

"Remember," Coach concluded, looking between them, "it's not about who has the most talent. It's about who's willing to do the work when it's hardest. Dismissed."

As they walked back to the locker room, Tyler was unusually quiet. Bear expected some resentment or defensiveness, but instead, Tyler finally said, "Coach was right. I cheated that last rep."

Bear didn't know how to respond, so he just nodded.

"I've been watching you, you know," Tyler continued. "How you're always the first one here, last one to leave. How you're getting better every day." He paused. "It's challenging me to step up my game."

Before Bear could respond, Tyler veered off toward his locker, leaving Bear to process what had just happened.

As Bear was leaving the locker room, Coach Turner called him over.

"Wilson. A word."

Bear approached, wondering if he was in trouble for confronting Akeem about the reps.

"Tony tells me you've been working hard this summer," Coach said, his expression neutral as always. "Says you're starting to understand what it takes."

Bear was caught off guard. "Yes, sir. I'm trying."

"Good." Coach nodded once, decisively. "Keep listening to him. Tony Brewer knows what he's talking about." He paused, then added, "And what you said to Johnson about the reps—you were right. That's the kind of leadership this team needs."

Before Bear could respond, Coach turned and walked away, leaving Bear standing there, processing the rare moment of approval.

Later, Bear found Akeem in the subdued locker room. Most players were too exhausted for their usual post-practice banter. As Bear gathered his things, Akeem approached, looking uncomfortable.

"Hey," Akeem said, keeping his voice low. "Sorry about before. You were right."

"About what?" Bear asked, though he knew.

"The reps. Cutting corners." Akeem sighed. "It's just, I never really thought it was a big deal, you know? I've always been fast enough and strong enough. Never really had to push beyond that."

Bear nodded, understanding. "I get it. But what if that's the difference between good and great? That extra push when everyone else is settling?"

"Maybe," Akeem admitted. "Anyway, I shouldn't have gotten defensive. That's on me."

"We're good," Bear assured him. "See you tomorrow?"

"Yeah. And Bear?" Akeem hesitated. "It won't happen again."

That evening, Bear stopped by the local library to return a book his mother had finished. As he waited at the checkout desk, he noticed Heather Chen sitting alone at a study table, surrounded by textbooks despite it being summer.

"Bear Wilson," the librarian called, sliding his mother's book across the counter. Her voice carried in the quiet space, causing Heather to look up. Their eyes met briefly, and she offered a polite smile before returning to her work.

Bear hesitated, then made a decision. He walked over to her table. "Hey, Heather, right? We have Mrs. Reynolds' English class together."

She looked up, slightly surprised. "Yes, Advanced English. You're doing the Gatsby essay too?"

"Trying to," Bear admitted with a small laugh. "Not exactly crushing it yet."

"It's challenging," she agreed. "I'm working on mine now, actually."

Bear nodded, suddenly aware that he'd interrupted her studying without having anything specific to say. "Well, I should let you get back to it. Just wanted to say hi."

"See you in class next month," she replied with another small smile.

As Bear left the library, he found himself thinking about Heather's dedication—studying intensely during summer break. It reminded him of what Tony had been saying about excellence in all areas. Maybe there were lessons to be learned beyond the football field.

When Bear got home, he helped his mom clear the dinner dishes. His phone buzzed with a text from an unknown number:

Wilson, didn't know you were gonna go all out on those hills. Had us all looking bad LOL. Thx for challenging me to step up tomorrow. —Greene

Bear stared at the message, surprised. He hadn't realized his example was having an impact on Tyler. Maybe leadership really wasn't about position but about actions—about making The Competitor's Choice consistently, even when it would be easier to drift.

His father came into the kitchen, noticing Bear's thoughtful expression. "Everything okay, son?"

"Yeah," Bear replied, showing him the text. "Just unexpected."

His dad read it and smiled. "That's how it works sometimes. You focus on doing the right thing, and others notice." He took a seat at the kitchen table. "Reminds me of something my high school running backs coach, Coach Gideon, used to say: 'Your actions speak so loudly, I can't hear what you're saying.'"

Bear sat down across from him. "I keep thinking about what Tony said—that this isn't really about me versus Tyler. That the real competition is me versus myself."

"Tony's a wise man," his father agreed. "Always was, even back in school."

"But it's hard sometimes," Bear admitted. "When I see Tyler cutting corners but still getting the starting spot because he's such a better athlete than me."

His father leaned forward. "Let me tell you something about talent versus discipline. Talent might get you in the door, but discipline keeps you in the room." He paused. "You know Michael Jordan?"

TALENT MIGHT GET YOU IN THE DOOR, BUT DISCIPLINE KEEPS YOU IN THE ROOM.

Bear rolled his eyes. "Of course, Dad."

"Did you know that when he was a freshman at North Carolina, he told his assistant coach, Roy Williams, that he wanted to be one of the best players in North Carolina history?"

Bear shook his head.

"Well, Coach Williams told him, 'You're going to have to work harder.' And Jordan was offended. He said, 'I work hard. I worked as hard as everyone else on my high school team.' And you know what Williams told him?"

"What?"

"He said, 'Yes, everyone on your high school team. But you talked about wanting to be one of the best here at one of the best basketball programs in the country. You're going to have to work harder because doing what everyone else does doesn't make you one of the best ever.'"1

The words hit Bear like a thunderbolt. If Michael Jordan—arguably the greatest basketball player ever—needed to hear that message, how much more did he need to take it to heart?

"So what you're saying is, it's not enough to just work as hard as Tyler."

His dad nodded. "If you want different results, you need different inputs. Exceptional outcomes require exceptional effort. Most people drift through life because they're only willing to do what everyone else does. Competitors—true competitors—are willing to do what others won't."

Bear thought about this as he went up to his room. All this time, he'd been measuring himself against Tyler Greene—trying to match Tyler's natural talent with hard work. But what if that was the wrong standard? What if the real question wasn't "Am I as good as Tyler?" but "Am I pushing beyond what everyone else is willing to do?"

In his journal that night, he wrote:

Today's Game: Standing up for the standard

My Competition: The desire to be liked vs. doing what's right

Why It Matters: Because cultures are built by what we accept

Today I spoke up when I saw a teammate cutting corners. It wasn't comfortable, but I'm starting to understand what Tony means about choices becoming habits and habits becoming character.

The Competitor's Choice: I'm seeing this everywhere now. When Akeem skipped reps, he was drifting. When Tyler didn't touch the line, he was drifting. Even when I almost let it slide to avoid an awkward conversation, I was tempted to drift too.

But maybe the most important thing I learned today is that Coach sees more than I thought. And Tyler's text surprised me completely. Maybe the "extra inch" isn't just about personal improvement, but also about raising the standard for everyone around you?

Still trying to figure out how all this fits together. But something is definitely changing—in me and maybe in the team too.

The next Saturday, Bear arrived early for his session with Tony. He found Tony already on the field, setting up cones for what looked like a complex footwork drill.

"Morning," Tony called. "Ready to work?"

"Always," Bear replied, dropping his bag on the sideline.

"Good. Because today we're going to talk about something important." Tony tossed him a football. "Tell me about yesterday's conditioning session."

Bear caught the ball, surprised by the question. "How did you know about that?"

"Small town," Tony said with a slight smile. "Word gets around."

Bear told him about the station training, the hill sprints, Akeem skipping reps, Tyler not touching the line, and Coach Turner calling them both out afterward. He also mentioned his conversation with Akeem and the unexpected text from Tyler.

Tony listened without interrupting, nodding occasionally. When Bear finished, he said, "So what's the lesson here?"

Bear thought for a moment. "That people notice when you do the right thing, even when you think no one's watching?"

"That's part of it," Tony agreed. "But there's something deeper. What's happening when you touch the line every time, complete every rep with purpose, even when you're tired and it would be easy to cut corners?"

"I'm building discipline," Bear suggested.

"Yes, but it's more than that. You're building identity." Tony picked up a cone and walked closer. "Every time you

EVERY TIME YOU TOUCH THE LINE, YOU'RE MAKING A STATEMENT—ABOUT WHO YOU ARE.

touch the line, you're making a statement—to yourself, more than anyone else—about who you are. You're saying, 'I'm the kind of person who does things right, who pushes through when it's hard, who maintains standards even when no one is watching.'"

He set the cone down precisely. "And every time you don't touch the line, you're also making a statement: 'I'm the kind of person who takes shortcuts, who settles for good enough, who only performs when others are watching.'"

Bear nodded, beginning to understand.

"The most powerful force in human psychology is the need to act in alignment with our identity," Tony continued. "If you see yourself as disciplined, you'll act disciplined. If you see yourself as exceptional, you'll act exceptional. But if you see yourself as average—as someone who does what everyone else does—guess how you'll perform?"

"Average," Bear said simply.

"Exactly. That's why touching the line matters so much. It's not just about the line itself—it's about who you become in the process of consistently touching it. It's about crossing the Ego Gap between who you are and who you could be."

Bear tossed the football back and forth between his hands, processing this insight. "So yesterday, when Coach called out Tyler for not touching the line—"

"He was really calling out who Tyler was becoming," Tony said, finishing Bear's thought. "And when he praised you for touching it, he was acknowledging who you're becoming."

"And that's why Tyler texted me," Bear said. "Because he saw the difference between who he was being and who I was being."

"Now you're getting it," Tony said approvingly. "Remember what we talked about with the one-degree difference? This is where it happens. In those moments when you're tired, when no one's watching, when it would be so easy to cut the corner. That's the one degree that transforms water to ice—or keeps it as just water."

He gestured toward the field. "Today, we're going to focus on building that identity—on strengthening your self-image as someone who goes beyond what's expected, who touches the line even when it's hard. *Especially* when it's hard."

CHAPTER 5
THE ACADEMIC CHALLENGE

As July moved toward August, the summer heat reached its peak in Jackson Creek. Football conditioning was in full swing, with daily workouts that left Bear physically drained but mentally sharp. The season opener was only a month away, and Bear was making steady progress in his sessions with Tony. But football wasn't his only challenge.

Bear stared at the blank document on his laptop screen, the cursor blinking accusingly. Two pages into his summer reading assignment for Advanced English, and he was already stuck.

He sighed, closing his laptop and flopping back on his bed. Football made sense to him. You practiced, you improved, you competed, you won or lost based on measurable performance. But how did you measure success in literary analysis? How did you know if your interpretation was "right"? Could

Tony's principles really help him here, or was he just not cut out for this?

English had never been his strongest subject. Bear was more comfortable with the concrete rules of math or the stories of history. The subjective nature of literary analysis—finding meaning where it wasn't explicitly stated—always left him feeling like he was guessing rather than knowing.

He'd signed up for Advanced English as a junior because his mother had encouraged him to challenge himself academically, not just athletically. "Colleges look at the whole picture," she'd reminded him. Now, as he struggled with this summer assignment due in three days when school started back, he was questioning that decision.

Sighing, Bear closed his laptop and flopped back on his bed. Football made sense to him. You practiced, you improved, you competed, you won or lost based on measurable performance. But how did you measure success in literary analysis? How did you know if your interpretation was "right"?

"Still wrestling with Gatsby?" his mother asked from the doorway, startling him.

"How'd you know?" Bear asked, pushing his laptop away.

Ellen Wilson smiled, entering his room and sitting on the edge of his bed. "I've been teaching long enough to recognize the look of English-essay frustration."

"I've read it twice," Bear said. "I understand the story, but all this symbolism analysis . . . it's just not clicking."

"That's because you're trying to find the 'right' answer," his mother suggested. "Literary analysis isn't like math, with clear-cut solutions. It's about developing your own interpretation and supporting it with evidence."

"That's the problem," Bear admitted. "How do I know if my interpretation is valid?"

His mother considered this. "Would it help to talk through some of your ideas? Sometimes verbalizing can clarify your thinking."

Bear hesitated. His mother was an English teacher, after all. But he'd always been reluctant to ask for her help with schoolwork, wanting to succeed on his own merits.

"Maybe later," he said finally. "I want to try working through it myself first."

His mother nodded, understanding. "My offer stands. And don't forget—you've got resources beyond me. That framework Tony's been teaching you for football . . . have you considered applying it to your academic challenges?"

The thought hadn't occurred to Bear. Could The Competitor's Choice apply to English essays as well as football drills?

EXCELLENCE ISN'T COMPARTMENTALIZED.

As if reading his thoughts, his mother added, "Excellence isn't compartmentalized, Bear. The principles that make someone great in one area often translate to others."

She sounded so much like Tony that Bear had to smile.

"I'll think about it," he promised.

After she left, Bear flopped back on his bed, mind working. Maybe she was right. Maybe he needed to approach this assignment the same way he'd been approaching his quarterback development—with a framework, with intentionality, with a willingness to push beyond his comfort zone.

His phone buzzed with a text from Tony: *How's the summer reading going?*

Bear blinked in surprise. How did Tony know about his English assignment? He typed back:

Struggling. How did you know?

Tony's reply came quickly: *Your mom mentioned it when I ran into her at the grocery store. Want to talk about it?*

Bear hesitated. The last few weeks had been focused on football—mechanics, film study, leadership. He wasn't sure how Tony's frameworks applied to something like English literature. But, then again, hadn't Tony said the principles of excellence applied to everything? He texted back: *Yes. When?*

Library. Two p.m. *Bring your book and notes.*

The Jackson Creek Public Library was a small but well-maintained building near the town square. Bear arrived a few minutes early, his copy of *The Great Gatsby* and a notebook tucked under his arm. He found Tony already seated at a table in the back, reading a book with the words "Mind Gym" on the front.

"Fitness?" Bear asked, nodding toward the book as he sat down.

"Mental fitness," Tony said, chuckling. Closing the book, he added, "Training the mind is just as important as training the body. I'm always looking to expand my own growth."

He gestured to Bear's book. "So, Gatsby's giving you trouble?"

Bear nodded, slightly embarrassed. "I've read it twice, and I get the basic story. Rich guy tries to win back his old girlfriend by throwing lavish parties and pretending to be something he's not.

"But when it comes to analyzing all the symbols and connecting them to modern society . . ." He trailed off, shrugging helplessly.

"What's your approach been so far?" Tony asked.

"I've been trying to identify all the symbols—the green light, the eyes of Doctor T.J. Eckleburg, the Valley of Ashes. Then I'm supposed to interpret what they represent and connect them to today's world. But it feels like I'm just guessing."

Tony nodded thoughtfully. "Sounds like you're approaching this the same way most students do: looking for the 'right' answers, as if literary analysis were a treasure hunt with predetermined Xs on the map."

"Isn't it?" Bear asked. "I mean, don't these symbols have specific meanings the author intended?"

"Sometimes," Tony acknowledged. "But often, the power of literature is that symbols can hold multiple meanings simultaneously, and those meanings can shift depending on the reader's perspective and the context in which they're reading."

Bear frowned. "That sounds convenient. Like there are no wrong answers."

Tony laughed. "Oh, there are definitely wrong answers. But there might be multiple right ones too." He leaned forward. "Let me ask you this: how have you been applying The Competitor's Choice framework to your football training?"

The sudden change in topic caught Bear off guard. "Well, I've been trying to make the choice to direct myself instead of drift. I've been focusing on competing against my own potential rather than just trying to beat Tyler. I've been touching the line, completing every rep with purpose. Basically, I've been following the COMPETE framework."

"Exactly," Tony said. "Now, how might you apply that same approach to this English assignment?"

Bear considered this for a moment. "I guess I'd need to clarify what game I'm playing first. Not just trying to get a good grade but really understanding the book and what it has to say."

"Good start," Tony said. "And the 'O' in COMPETE?"

"Observe the rules of excellence," Bear replied. "I'd need to understand what makes a great literary analysis, not just an adequate one."

Tony nodded. "Which might mean going beyond just identifying symbols and their possible meanings. It might mean connecting them to the novel's themes, to historical context, to your own experience as a reader."

Bear was starting to see the parallels. "And for 'M'—model the best—I'd need to look at examples of great literary analysis. See how other people have approached similar assignments."

"Now you're getting it," Tony said. "Just like when we watched film of elite quarterbacks to understand what separates them, you can study excellent literary analysis to see what makes it compelling."

He tapped Bear's copy of Gatsby. "Here's another way to think about it: When you're facing a tough defense, do you just focus on their personnel? Or do you look for patterns, tendencies, opportunities?"

"Patterns and tendencies," Bear answered. "So I can anticipate what they'll do in different situations."

"Apply that same thinking to the novel," Tony suggested. "Don't just identify isolated symbols. Look for patterns, connections, recurring themes—just like you'd look for defensive tendencies that create opportunities."

Tony leaned back in his chair. "Let's try a different approach. Forget about what you think you're 'supposed' to find in the novel. Instead, tell me: What struck you most about the story? What stayed with you after you finished reading?"

Bear thought about it. "The green light at the end of Daisy's dock. Gatsby staring at it from across the bay. It's like he's so close to his dream, but he's also so far away. And no matter how rich he gets, how many parties he throws, he can't quite reach it."

"That's good," Tony said. "Now ask yourself: where do you see that same dynamic in today's world? Where do people chase dreams that remain just out of reach, no matter how much external success they achieve?"

Bear's mind immediately went to social media—people presenting carefully curated versions of their lives, always striving for more likes, more followers, more validation.

"Instagram," he said. "People showing off the perfect life that isn't really perfect. Chasing approval that never quite satisfies."

"There you go," Tony said with a smile. "That's a connection with depth and insight. Not just 'the green light represents hope' but a specific application to modern society that demonstrates true understanding." He gestured to Bear's notebook. "Try that approach with the other symbols. Don't worry about being 'right' at first. Just be authentic and thoughtful."

For the next hour, they worked through the major symbols in the novel, with Tony asking probing questions that helped Bear develop his own interpretations and connections. By the time they finished, Bear had three pages of notes and a much clearer direction for his essay.

"This is really helpful," Bear said, reviewing what they'd accomplished. "But I still don't understand why you're doing this. You're teaching me about football, not English."

"Am I?" Tony retorted. "Or am I teaching you about excellence, which applies everywhere?" He closed Bear's book. "Remember The Competitor's Choice diagram? Default Outcomes versus Desired Outcomes? Most students drift through assignments like this—doing the minimum, looking for the easiest interpretation, cutting corners mentally."

He tapped the book. "But competitors make a different choice. They cross the Ego Gap by being willing to think deeply, to form authentic interpretations, to put in the mental effort when most people won't. In football, you're learning to touch the line when no one's watching. In academics, it's about pushing beyond surface-level analysis when the easy C+ is right there for the taking. Different fields, same mindset."

Bear nodded slowly, understanding. "One degree. The difference between water and ice."

"Exactly," Tony confirmed. "Most students approach assignments like this looking for the minimum effort to get by—what's the least I need to do to get a passing grade? But you're not most students anymore, are you?"

"Not anymore," Bear replied with growing conviction.

"Good. Now here's your challenge: I want you to approach this essay with the same intensity, focus, and commitment to excellence that you bring to the football field. Imagine it's fourth down, state championship on the line. What kind of effort would you give?"

"Everything I have," Bear said without hesitation.

"Then do the same here," Tony said, standing to leave. "And Bear? When you finish, I want you to share it with someone else struggling with the same assignment. The final 'E' in COMPETE is *Environment*. You elevate others by elevating yourself."

"Whom should I share it with?" Bear asked.

Tony smiled. "I'll leave that to you to figure out. But remember, leadership isn't about position: it's about action."

As they walked out of the library, Bear felt a new sense of purpose about the assignment. He'd been approaching it all wrong—seeing it as an obstacle to endure rather than a challenge to embrace, just like Sisyphus with his boulder.

"One more thing," Tony said as they reached the parking lot. "Remember what happens when you touch the line consistently in one area of your life?"

"It becomes easier to touch it in others," Bear answered.

"Exactly. Excellence isn't compartmentalized; it's a mindset that transfers across domains. Every time you choose direction over drift in one area, you strengthen your ability to make that same choice everywhere else."

That evening, Bear worked on his essay with newfound purpose. Instead of trying to guess what his teacher wanted to hear, he focused on developing his own authentic interpreta-

EVERY TIME YOU CHOOSE DIRECTION OVER DRIFT IN ONE AREA, YOU STRENGTHEN YOUR ABILITY TO MAKE THAT SAME CHOICE EVERYWHERE ELSE.

tions, supporting them with evidence from the text, and making meaningful connections to the world he lived in.

He approached the work like a quarterback studying film—looking for patterns, making connections, developing insights that weren't immediately obvious. He treated each paragraph like a rep, giving it full focus and purpose.

When he finally finished, well past midnight, Bear had written not just the required five pages but eight. More importantly, he felt a sense of ownership and pride in what he'd created—not because it would earn him a good grade (though he suspected it would), but because it represented his best thinking and his authentic voice.

The next morning, Bear reread his essay, made a few final edits, and then faced Tony's final challenge: sharing it with someone else struggling with the same assignment. As he considered who might benefit, he remembered seeing a girl from his class at the library several times over the summer, always surrounded by books. Though they'd never really talked beyond occasional group work in class, she was clearly serious about academics. But he now couldn't remember her name.

He looked her up in the class directory—Heather Chen. They'd had several Advanced English and math classes together, where she was always front row, hand always raised with the right answer. He'd admired her intelligence from afar but never really had a reason to connect.

He found her email in the class directory and sent her a message:

Heather,

We're in Advanced English together. I know we haven't talked much, but I've been struggling with the Gatsby essay and had a breakthrough yesterday. I'm attaching my draft—not because I think it's perfect, but because sharing perspectives might help us both develop stronger analyses.

If you want to talk through ideas or exchange feedback, let me know. No pressure either way.

—Bear

He attached his essay and hit send before he could second-guess himself. It felt vulnerable, sharing work that was still in progress, especially with someone as academically gifted as Heather. But wasn't that part of what Tony had been teaching him? Being willing to cross the Ego Gap by risking failure in pursuit of improvement?

To his surprise, Heather responded within an hour:

Bear,

Thanks for sharing your essay. I've been stuck on mine for days! Your analysis of the green light is really insightful—I hadn't considered the social media parallel at all.

I've attached my draft too. It's only three pages so far, but I have some different interpretations that might complement yours.

Would you want to meet at Jackson Creek Coffee tomorrow at 10 a.m. to discuss? Two brains are better than one!

—Heather

Bear smiled as he read her response. Maybe he had more to offer academically than he'd realized. And perhaps this was the beginning of a new connection . . . someone who could challenge him intellectually the way Tyler challenged him athletically.

The next day, he met Heather at the coffee shop, and they spent two hours comparing interpretations and refining their arguments. By the time they finished, both had stronger essays than when they started.

"You know, I was surprised when I got your email," Heather admitted as they packed up their laptops. "I didn't think football players cared this much about English essays."

Bear laughed. "I'm learning that excellence isn't compartmentalized. Someone's been teaching me that the same mindset that creates success in one area can transfer to others."

"Who taught you that?" Heather asked curiously.

"Tony Brewer," Bear replied. "He's been mentoring me this summer."

Heather's eyebrows rose. "*The* Tony Brewer? State championship quarterback Tony Brewer?"

"That's him," Bear confirmed. "Though he's teaching me about a lot more than just football. He has this framework called COMPETE and this concept called The Competitor's Choice."

As Bear explained Tony's philosophy, he realized how much he'd internalized in just a few weeks. The principles that had seemed abstract at first were now becoming second nature, guiding not just his approach to football but to other areas of his life.

One week later, Bear checked his email and found a message from Mrs. Cummins regarding the summer reading assignments. The Advanced English teacher had required all students to submit their essays electronically before the school year began, giving her time to review their work and assess their writing levels.

Bear clicked on the message, his stomach tightening slightly. The subject line read *Summer Essay Feedback—Wilson, Barrett.*

He opened the email to find his essay attached with comments throughout, and at the top of the first page was an A along with a note:

Exceptional analysis. You've made thoughtful connections to contemporary issues. Great work; look forward to seeing more of your work in class this year.

Bear smiled as he read the comment. It was his first A in English since elementary school.

That evening at dinner, Bear shared his essay grade with his parents, trying to sound casual despite his excitement.

"An A in Advanced English?" his father asked, pride evident in his voice. "That's impressive, son."

"Mrs. Cummins said it was 'strong work,'" Bear added, unable to keep the satisfaction from his tone.

His mother smiled knowingly. "I'm not surprised. I could tell something had shifted in your approach when you were working on it."

"I tried applying what Tony's been teaching me," Bear explained. "Clarifying what game I was playing—not just getting a grade but really understanding the book. Observing what makes great literary analysis. Modeling examples of excellent work."

"The COMPETE framework," his father noted.

"Yeah," Bear confirmed. "It's weird how well it transferred from football to academics."

"Not weird at all," his mother said. "The principles of excellence are universal. They're about how you approach challenges, not what specific challenges you face."

His father nodded. "That's what separates the truly successful from the merely talented in any field: the ability to apply disciplined frameworks across domains."

Bear thought about this as he helped clear the dishes. His parents had been teaching him these principles all along, in their own ways. His father's meticulous attention to customer details at the auto store. His mother's thoughtful engagement with her students' work. They had been modeling excellence in the margins, touching the line when no one was watching.

"Thanks," he said suddenly, looking at both his parents.

"For what?" his mother asked.

"For pushing me to take Advanced English even though I didn't want to," Bear answered. "For believing I could do more than just 'get by' in subjects that don't come naturally to me."

His parents exchanged a look—one of those wordless communications that Bear had observed throughout his childhood.

"That's our job," his father said simply. "To see potential you might not see in yourself yet."

Later, as Bear prepared for bed, he realized that his parents and Tony were doing essentially the same thing: helping him go from default outcomes to desired ones. The only difference was the specific arena in which they were guiding him.

As he recorded the experience in his journal, Bear wrote:

Today's Game: Applying excellence to academics

My Competition: The part of me that settles for "good enough" in subjects that don't come naturally

Why It Matters: Because excellence isn't compartmentalized—it's who you are, not just what you do in one area.

The Competitor's Choice: Today I realized that touching the line isn't just a football concept. It's about giving your best effort in everything you do, especially when it would be easy to cut corners.

When you touch the line in one area of life, it becomes easier to touch it in others. Excellence becomes a habit, a mindset, an identity that crosses the Ego Gap in every domain.

As he closed his journal, Bear realized something important: His competition with Tyler Greene for the starting quarterback position was no longer his sole focus. It still mattered, of course—he still wanted to win the job—but he wasn't obsessing over Tyler every second of every day as he had once been.

Instead, he was competing against himself, pushing to become the best version of himself in every arena. And in that competition, there were victories to be won every day, regardless of what happened on the football field.

With just a few weeks left before school started, Bear felt more prepared than ever—not just for football, but for all the challenges ahead.

CHAPTER 6
CLASSROOM STRUGGLES

The first day of school arrived in late August, bringing with it the familiar mix of excitement and dread that marked the end of summer freedom. The hallways of Jackson Creek High School buzzed with activity as students compared schedules and caught up on summer adventures. Football practices were now in full swing, with the season opener just three weeks away. Bear was still officially the backup quarterback, but the gap between him and Tyler had narrowed over the summer. Coach Turner had even started giving Bear reps with the first-team offense occasionally, a sign that his hard work was beginning to pay off.

As Bear navigated the crowded hallway toward his locker, he noticed a group of freshmen huddled nervously by the gym entrance, clearly intimidated by their first day of high school. Among them was a familiar face: Max Jenkins, the lanky middle schooler Bear had spotted watching his practice sessions with Tony over the summer. Max stood out from his peers, carrying himself with the confident posture of an athlete rather than the tentative stance of a typical freshman.

Coach Turner passed by, nodding briefly to Bear before stopping to speak with Max. Their conversation was brief, but the coach's body language—the firm handshake, the attentive stance—suggested he saw something promising in the young quarterback. Bear made a mental note to watch the freshman team's first practice. If the rumors about Max's arm talent were true, Jackson Creek's quarterback pipeline might be stronger than he'd realized.

Bear's new class schedule included all the usual subjects, plus one he'd been dreading: chemistry. Science had never been his strongest suit, and he'd heard that Mrs. Gowin was one of the toughest teachers in school.

"Don't worry about it," Akeem said as they compared schedules in the hallway before first period. "I heard she curves the grades. Just don't be at the bottom of the class."

Bear frowned. That approach didn't sit well with him anymore. Over the summer, working with Tony, he'd started to see how the principles they discussed applied beyond football.

"That's not good enough," Bear replied. "I don't want to just get by."

Akeem raised an eyebrow. "Since when are you gunning for top grades in science?"

"I'm really learning that excellence isn't compartmentalized," Bear said, echoing Tony's words. "Either you give your best in everything, or you're just pretending in some areas."

EITHER YOU GIVE YOUR BEST IN EVERYTHING, OR YOU'RE JUST PRETENDING IN SOME AREAS.

"Whatever you say, Professor Wilson," Akeem said with a laugh, nudging Bear's shoulder. "But don't come crying to me when you're drowning in chemical equations and valence electrons."

When Bear walked into chemistry class third period, Mrs. Gowin was already writing equations on the board. She was a small woman with short white hair and glasses perched on the end of her nose, but she had an intimidating presence that immediately quieted the room.

"Welcome to chemistry," she said without preamble. "This class will challenge you. Some of you will struggle. All of you will work harder than you think you're capable of."

Her eyes scanned the room, pausing briefly on Bear, who shifted uncomfortably in his seat.

"We'll start with a test to see what you remember from biology last year," she announced, passing out papers. "This won't count toward your grade, but it will tell me what I'm working with."

The test was brutal. Bear stared at questions about molecular structures and chemical reactions, recognizing almost nothing. By the time he turned in his paper, his confidence was shaken. This wasn't just difficult; it was like trying to read a foreign language he'd never been exposed to.

That evening, Bear sat at the kitchen table, the chemistry textbook open before him, his frustration mounting with each incomprehensible paragraph.

"Having trouble?" his father asked, setting down a cup of coffee next to Bear's notebook.

"I don't even know where to start," Bear admitted. "It's like everything builds on concepts I'm supposed to already understand, but I don't."

His father pulled up a chair. "Your mom mentioned you were worried about this class. Let me see if I can help. Chemistry was actually my best subject in high school."

Bear looked up in surprise. "It was?"

"Hard to believe, I know," his father said, chuckling. "The auto parts guy being a science nerd. But the principles of chemistry apply directly to engines—fuel combustion, material properties, fluid dynamics."

He flipped to the first chapter, scanning the content. "Look, the periodic table is like a playbook. Each element has specific properties and behaviors, just like each player has their position and role. Once you understand the patterns, it starts to make sense."

For the next thirty minutes, his father walked him through some of the basic concepts, translating the academic language into practical examples from car engines and everyday life. By the time they finished, Bear hadn't mastered the material, but he at least had a foothold—a way to start making sense of the intimidating terminology.

"Thanks, Dad," Bear said, genuinely grateful. "That helps."

"You know," his father said, standing to leave, "your mother and I have been watching you apply Tony's frameworks to football, then to English. Now you're facing chemistry. Each new challenge is an opportunity to prove those principles work universally—that excellence isn't domain-specific, but character-driven."

Bear nodded, the connection becoming clearer. "Touching the line in subjects that don't come naturally."

"Exactly," his father confirmed. "And remember: Asking for help isn't weakness. It's strategic. Even the best quarter-backs need receivers, linemen, and coaches."

Bear's phone buzzed with a text from Tony: *How was the first day?*

Bear hesitated, then typed back: *Football good. Chemistry awful.*

Three dots appeared, then Tony's words flashed across Bear's screen: *Sounds like we need to talk. Hardware store Saturday, 7 a.m.?*

Bear agreed, then turned back to his textbook with a sigh. He tried reading the first section again, taking notes as he went, but the concepts remained a foreign language.

Finally, he closed the book and pulled out his journal. He hadn't been as consistent with his entries in the last week, but tonight he felt the need to process his thoughts:

Today's Game: Facing a challenge (chemistry) that doesn't come naturally to me

My Competition: The temptation to give up or look for shortcuts when things get hard

Why It Matters: Because I don't want to start accepting "just good enough" in one area of my life when it gets hard

Bear closed his journal, still not sure how he was going to tackle chemistry, but somehow feeling better for having named the challenge.

The first week of school flew by, and Tony was waiting at the hardware store when Bear arrived Saturday morning. They settled into the back office, and Tony could immediately see the frustration on Bear's face.

"Tell me about chemistry," Tony said.

Bear explained his struggles with the class, how even on the first day he felt completely lost, and how he was worried about even being able to pass the class.

"You know," Tony said after listening carefully, "we've been focusing on the 'M' in COMPETE: *Modeling Excellence.* But now it's time to talk about the 'P'—*Position*: Own Your Starting Line."

He pointed to the whiteboard where the framework was still written. "Before you can move forward, you have to honestly assess where you're starting from. No excuses, no comparisons to others. Just the truth about where you stand right now."

Bear frowned. "So I need to accept that I'm terrible at science?"

"Not exactly," Tony said. "You need to accept that science doesn't come naturally to you, and that you're starting from behind. But that doesn't determine where you'll finish."

He leaned forward. "Tell me something: when you first started playing quarterback, were you immediately good at reading defenses?"

"No way," Bear admitted. "It was overwhelming. All the different coverages, trying to make decisions in split seconds."

"But you got better," Tony observed. "How?"

Bear thought about it. "Practice. Watching film. Asking questions. Learning from my mistakes."

"Exactly," Tony said. "You applied a process to improve. Now you need to do the same thing with chemistry."

He grabbed a marker and wrote *TODAY* on the whiteboard. "This is how you'll tackle chemistry . . . and any other challenge that comes your way."

Bear studied the new framework:

T- TIMING: MASTER YOUR SEASON
O- OBLIGATIONS: HONOR COMMITMENTS, MAINTAIN MOMENTUM
D- DREAM: CONNECT TO YOUR "WHY"
A- ATTITUDE: CHOOSE YOUR COMPETITIVE EDGE
Y- YOU VS. YOU: BEAT YESTERDAY'S BEST

"The TODAY framework is about executing your strategy for today's battle," Tony explained. "Most people get caught up by looking too far ahead and then getting paralyzed by the gap between where they are and where they want to go.

"But big goals are achieved through small actions we take every 'today' we have."

He pointed to the "T" first. "*Timing*: Master Your Season. First, you need to recognize what season you're in. Right now, you're in a learning season for chemistry. Your expectations need to match your reality."

"So I shouldn't expect to get an A?" Bear asked.

"Not immediately," Tony said. "But you should expect yourself to improve every day. The goal isn't perfection—it's progress."

He moved to the "O."

YOU SHOULD EXPECT YOURSELF TO IMPROVE EVERY DAY.

"*Obligations*: Honor Commitments, Maintain Momentum. You need to prioritize with purpose. Block time for what matters most."

"Like studying chemistry," Bear said.

"Exactly. Schedule it when your mind is fresh, not when you're exhausted from practice. Make it nonnegotiable."

Moving to the "D," Tony continued, "*Dream*: Connect to Your Why. What's your purpose for doing well in chemistry beyond just passing the class?"

Bear had to think about that one. "Well, I want to keep my eligibility for football. And I guess learning how to tackle something that's hard for me will make me stronger overall."

"Good," Tony said. "Always connect today's effort to your bigger vision."

"The 'A' stands for *Attitude*: Choose Your Competitive Edge," Tony explained. "Your attitude is one hundred percent your choice. You can approach chemistry as a burden or as a challenge to overcome."

"And the 'Y'?" Bear asked.

"*You vs. You:* Beat Yesterday's Best," Tony said. "The only real competition is internal. Each day, try to understand one more concept than you did the day before. Progress compounds over time."

Bear nodded, starting to see how he could apply these principles to his chemistry class. "So it's about touching the line in the classroom too."

"Everything is connected," Tony confirmed. "The discipline to do the right thing, even when it's hard, applies everywhere in life."

As Bear left the hardware store, his mind was already working on a plan for tackling chemistry. He'd approach it the same way he approached football—not trying to become a chemistry genius overnight, but making incremental progress each day.

The next day in chemistry, when Mrs. Gowin announced they would be working in lab pairs for the semester, Bear immediately raised his hand.

"Mrs. Gowin, would it be possible for me to work with someone who's strong in chemistry? I'm starting from behind, and I really want to improve."

The class went quiet, surprised by Bear's candor. Mrs. Gowin looked equally surprised.

"That's refreshing honesty, Mr. Wilson," she said. "I'll pair you with Heather Chen. She had the highest score on the diagnostic test."

Heather, who was sitting in the front row, turned and gave Bear a small smile.

After class, he approached her. "Thanks for being my lab partner. I should warn you, I'm pretty lost already."

Heather adjusted her glasses. "That's okay. Chemistry makes sense to me. Maybe I can help you see it differently."

"I'd appreciate that," Bear replied sincerely. "I'm willing to put in the work. I just need someone to point me in the right direction."

"Well," Heather said, seeming to make a decision, "I have study hall fourth period. If you're free then, we could go over the first chapter together in the library."

Bear's fourth period was his lunch break, but he nodded immediately. "That would be great. I'll bring my lunch to the library."

When Bear met Heather in the library that day, he was fully prepared. He'd spent the previous evening reading the first chapter again, highlighting confusing sections and writing down specific questions. He'd even watched a few YouTube videos on basic chemistry concepts, though they hadn't entirely made sense to him.

"Wow," Heather said, looking at his notes. "You really are serious about this."

"I am," Bear confirmed. "I'm applying the same approach I use for football: identify my weaknesses, create a plan, and put in the work to improve."

Heather smiled. "I've never heard anyone talk about studying for a class that way before. Most people just try to get by."

"I used to be like that," Bear admitted. "But I'm learning that how you do one thing is how you do everything."

For the next thirty minutes, Heather patiently walked Bear through the basic concepts of atoms, molecules, and chemical bonds, using analogies that made the complex ideas more concrete. She explained valence electrons as "social atoms" that wanted to make friends by sharing or giving away electrons. By the end of their session, Bear felt like he had a foothold in the material for the first time.

"This was really helpful," he told her as they packed up. "Could we do this again tomorrow?"

"Sure," Heather said. "But don't you want to eat lunch with your friends?"

Bear thought about it. "My priority right now is understanding chemistry. Besides, my friends will understand."

That evening, Akeem texted him: *Where were u at lunch? Missed the QB at the table.*

Bear replied honestly: *Study session for chemistry. Trying to get ahead of it before I fall behind.*

Akeem sent back a laughing emoji and wrote: *Nerd alert! But respect, man. Do what you gotta do.*

When Bear mentioned his chemistry study sessions to his mother, she seemed both surprised and pleased.

"Heather Chen is helping you?" she asked. "She's brilliant. Her mother teaches at the community college, I think."

"She explains things in a way that actually makes sense," Bear said. "And she doesn't make me feel stupid for asking basic questions."

"That's the mark of someone who truly understands a subject," his mother observed. "They can make complex ideas accessible to others."

"I wish I had that gift," Bear said, sighing. "Everything in my head makes sense until I try to explain it to someone else."

"That's a skill you can develop," his mother replied. "In fact, teaching others is one of the best ways to deepen your own understanding."

The next day, Bear met Heather in the library again. This time, she'd brought molecular model kits—plastic balls and sticks that could be assembled to represent different molecules.

"I thought this might help," she explained. "Sometimes seeing and touching the structures makes them easier to understand than just looking at diagrams in the textbook."

Bear picked up a red ball. "Oxygen?"

"Yes," Heather confirmed, looking impressed. "And the black ones are carbon, white is hydrogen."

"So water would be . . . " Bear assembled one red ball with two white ones.

"Perfect," Heather said. "H_2O. And methane would be . . ."

Bear thought for a moment, then put together one black ball with four white ones.

"CH_4?" he asked.

"You're getting it," Heather said with a smile.

For the rest of the period, they built increasingly complex molecules, with Heather explaining the concepts as they worked. The hands-on approach made the abstract concepts more real in a way the textbook never could.

"You know," Heather said as they were wrapping up, "you shouldn't sell yourself short on chemistry. You're picking this up faster than most people would."

"I have a good teacher," Bear replied.

Heather blushed slightly. "Well, I have a confession. I struggle with English lit. That Gatsby essay you shared over the summer really helped me more than you realize. I felt so stuck! So I guess this makes us even."

The daily study sessions continued, and slowly but surely, the foreign language of chemistry began to make sense. By the end of the third week, Bear was able to complete homework assignments without constantly referring to the textbook or his notes.

Heather noticed his progress too. "You're asking different questions now," she observed during one session. "Not 'what does this mean?' but 'why does this happen?' That's a good sign."

When Mrs. Gowin handed back their first quiz, Bear held his breath as he turned the paper over. C-. Not great, but not the F he had feared. And more importantly, he understood why he had missed the questions he got wrong.

He showed the quiz to Heather at their next study session.

"That's actually pretty good for a first quiz," she said encouragingly. "Mrs. Gowin's tests are notoriously difficult."

By the third quiz, Bear had improved to a B-. He was starting to see patterns in the material, connections between different concepts. It wasn't just memorization anymore—he was developing an actual understanding of the subject.

More importantly, the process of tackling chemistry had reinforced everything Tony had been teaching him about discipline, perseverance, and touching the line even when—especially when—things were difficult.

One afternoon, as they were finishing up a study session, Heather asked, "I've heard you mention a few times this 'excellence can't be compartmentalized' mindset. Where did you learn that?"

"Tony Brewer," Bear replied. "He's been mentoring me since this summer."

"That's right. You did tell me this summer he was helping you." Heather asked.

"I thought we'd only talk football, but he's been teaching more than I expected. He has these frameworks—COMPETE and TODAY—that apparently apply to everything."

Heather looked intrigued. "What do they stand for?"

Bear explained the frameworks, surprised at how easily the concepts flowed now. They had become part of how he thought about challenges, whether on the field, in the classroom, or elsewhere.

"That's actually really interesting," Heather said when he finished. "Do you think . . . could it help with other subjects too? Like English?"

"Definitely," Bear assured her. "That's how I approached our Gatsby essay—clarifying what game I was playing, observing the rules of excellence, modeling the best examples I could find."

Heather seemed to consider this. "Would you mind . . . I mean, if you have time . . . maybe we could study English together sometimes too? I could keep helping you with chemistry, and you could help me with Mrs. Cummins' class?"

"I'd like that," Bear said, surprised to realize how much he meant it. Heather's intelligence and dedication were qualities he had come to admire. And he was beginning to see that he had something valuable to offer as well—a framework for approaching challenges that applied to more than just football.

As Bear walked to football practice that afternoon, he thought about how much his perspective had changed in just a few months. Last spring, he had been singularly focused on beating Tyler Greene for the starting quarterback position. Chemistry would have been viewed as an annoying obstacle, something to endure rather than improve at.

Now, he approached both football and chemistry with the same mindset—not trying to be the best in comparison to others, but continually improving to become the best version of himself. And in that process, he was building confidence in what he was truly capable of achieving.

In his journal that night, Bear wrote:

Today's Game: Applying strategic frameworks to academic challenges

My Competition: The instinct to surrender when faced with unfamiliar territory

Why It Matters: Because excellence requires consistency across all domains, not selective effort

TODAY:

T—Timing: I'm in a learning season for chemistry. Initial struggles don't predict final outcomes.

O—Obligations: Scheduled dedicated study blocks when my mind is freshest, not after practice.

D—Dream: Connected chemistry success to my larger goals of being complete, not compartmentalized.

A—Attitude: Chose curiosity over frustration, seeing this as a puzzle to solve rather than an obstacle.

Y—You vs. You: Today I understood valence electrons better than I did yesterday. Progress compounds.

The frameworks Tony has been teaching me aren't just football concepts—they're life strategies. By repositioning myself honestly and owning my starting line in chemistry without excuses, I created space for growth instead of frustration.

What's becoming clear is that touching the line isn't about being naturally good at everything. It's about bringing the same intentionality and discipline to every challenge, especially the ones that don't come easily. My competition isn't Heather or anyone else in the class—it's the version of myself that wants to settle for "good enough" in subjects that aren't my strength.

I'm beginning to see connections. The same mental toughness that pushes me through hill sprints can push me through chemical equations. The focus that helps me read defensive coverages can help me understand molecular structures. Excellence isn't compartmentalized—it's integrated.

Bear closed his journal, feeling a sense of quiet confidence. He was not just competing but becoming.

And that, he was beginning to understand, was the real victory.

CHAPTER 7
BUILDING BONDS

"Dude, are you ever around anymore?"

Akeem's question caught Bear off guard as they warmed up before afternoon practice. It had been a particularly grueling week—daily football practices, chemistry quizzes, and his regular sessions with Tony had left little time for anything else.

"What do you mean?" Bear asked, though he had a pretty good idea.

"I mean, you're like a ghost," Akeem said, stretching his hamstrings. "Some mysterious morning meetings with Tony, lunch in the library with Heather, practice, then straight home to study. The guys wanted to hit up Jackson Creek Pizza last night, but you didn't even respond to the group text."

Bear winced, remembering the notification he'd seen and promptly forgotten as he had been working through homework.

"Sorry about that. I've been focused on—"

"Yeah, yeah . . . competing, touching the line, being excellent, and all that," Akeem interrupted. "But, man, football's supposed to be a priority, not to mention your teammates, too. Team bonding and all that."

Coach Turner's whistle cut through the air before Bear could respond, but Akeem's words lingered. As they split into position groups, Bear noticed Akeem's own distraction—he was checking his phone between drills, his mind clearly elsewhere.

Later, as they ran routes against air, Bear pulled Akeem aside.

"Everything good?" he asked. "You seem distracted today."

Akeem hesitated. "My mom's working double shifts at the hospital this week. I'm supposed to watch my little sister after practice, but my cousins wanted me to go to the movies tonight."

"Sounds like your own balancing act," Bear observed.

"Yeah," Akeem admitted with a short laugh. "I get on you about team time, but I'm juggling just as much. Family, football, school, social life—something's always gotta give."

This glimpse into Akeem's struggles gave Bear a new perspective. Everyone was fighting their own battle with balance, not just him.

The comment stung, partly because Bear knew Akeem was right. He'd been so focused on improving himself, on touching the line in every aspect of his life, that he'd forgotten the importance of his relationships. But how could he balance it all? How could he be a great quarterback, a decent student, and a good friend without something slipping through the cracks? Did Tony's principles apply to his personal life, or were they just for the field and the classroom?

Coach Turner's whistle saved him from having to respond. "Offense, defense: separate! Let's get moving!"

Throughout practice, Akeem's words kept replaying in Bear's mind. He was throwing well, making good reads, but something felt off. The connection with his receivers, the camaraderie with his linemen—it wasn't as strong as it had been. He'd been so focused on his individual excellence that he'd neglected the team aspect of the game.

After practice, Bear lingered in the locker room longer than usual, joining in the banter instead of rushing off to study. When Tyler mentioned a video game tournament at his house on Saturday, Bear surprised everyone by saying, "Count me in."

"For real?" Akeem asked skeptically. "No extra throwing sessions or chemistry equations?"

"For real," Bear confirmed. "I could use a break."

The next morning, Bear arrived early for his session with Tony. As he approached the field, he spotted Tony and Tyler in conversation near the far sideline. They weren't practicing, just talking, Tony's hand occasionally landing on Tyler's shoulder for emphasis. They nodded to each other before Tyler jogged away, giving Bear a brief nod as they passed.

"Morning," Bear said to Tony, trying to sound casual. "Tyler's here early."

"He had some questions about leadership," Tony replied, not elaborating further. "Ready to work?"

Bear pushed down his curiosity and focused on the session, but the image of Tony and Tyler deep in conversation stayed with him. The mentor he'd come to think of as exclusively his seemed to be sharing his wisdom more broadly than Bear had realized.

"Something on your mind?" he asked as they took a water break.

Bear hesitated, then explained Akeem's comments and his realization that he might be neglecting the teammate aspects of football—and life in general.

"Ah," Tony said, nodding thoughtfully. "We've covered most of the COMPETE framework, but we haven't talked much about the final 'E'—*Environment*: Choose Your Circle, Change Your Ceiling."

"What does that mean exactly?"

"It means the people and influences around you determine your growth potential," Tony explained. "But it's not just about surrounding yourself with excellence. It's also about contributing to others' growth, building relationships that elevate everyone involved."

Bear considered this. "So it's not enough to just focus on my own improvement? I need to think about my teammates too?"

THE PEOPLE AND INFLUENCES AROUND YOU DETERMINE YOUR GROWTH POTENTIAL.

"Exactly," Tony confirmed. "Think about it: Even if you become the most technically perfect quarterback Jackson Creek has ever seen, if your receivers don't trust you, if your linemen don't believe in you, if your teammates don't want to follow you, what good is all that individual excellence?"

The question hit home. Bear had been so focused on his personal competition against himself that he'd forgotten football was ultimately a team sport.

"But how do I balance it?" Bear asked. "There are only so many hours in a day. If I'm spending time hanging out, that's time I'm not improving."

Tony smiled. "That's where you're making a false distinction. Building relationships isn't separate from excellence—it's part of it. Especially for a quarterback."

He picked up a football and tossed it to Bear. "The greatest quarterbacks in history weren't just technically skilled, they were leaders who brought out the best in everyone around them. They understood that their job wasn't just to improve themselves, but to elevate their teammates."

"So touching the line in relationships means—" Bear trailed off, trying to connect the concepts.

"It means giving the same attention, intention, and effort to your relationships that you give to your throwing mechanics or your chemistry homework," Tony said, driving the point home. "It means not cutting corners with people, even when you're tired or busy. It means being fully present with whoever you're with, instead of mentally rehearsing plays or chemical formulas."

Bear nodded slowly, understanding dawning. "I've been compartmentalizing again, haven't I? Treating relationships as separate from my pursuit of excellence."

"We all do it," Tony acknowledged. "It's easier to measure progress in tangible areas—how far you can throw, what grade you get on a quiz. Relationship quality is harder to quantify, so we often neglect it when we're busy."

"So what do I do?" Bear asked. "I can't just drop everything else."

"No, but you can apply the same frameworks," Tony said. "Clarify what game you're playing—not just being a good athlete or student, but being a good friend, teammate, and leader. Observe the rules of excellence in relationships—being present, listening actively, supporting others' goals as much as your own."

He continued moving through the framework. "Model the best—who are the leaders you admire for their ability to connect with others? Position yourself honestly—recognize where your relationship skills need work. Execute with purpose—be intentional about the time you spend with others, making it count. Take time to reflect on your interactions. And create an environment that brings out the best in everyone."

Bear thought about the video game tournament at Tyler's house. It had seemed like a distraction from his goals, but now he was seeing it differently—as an opportunity to build connections, to strengthen the team bonds that would ultimately make them all better.

"And don't forget the TODAY framework," Tony added. "*Timing*—recognize that there are seasons for intense individual focus and seasons for relationship building. *Obligations*—

honor your commitments to others, not just to your own improvement. *Dream*—connect to your why, which should include the people you care about. *Attitude*—approach relationships with the same positive mindset you bring to football. And *You vs. You*—try to be a better friend, teammate, and leader today than you were yesterday."

As Bear drove home, he thought about how to apply these principles practically. He couldn't abandon his academic or athletic pursuits, but he could be more intentional about the time he did spend with others.

That afternoon, instead of heading straight to the library during lunch, Bear joined his teammates at their usual table. Heather spotted him from across the cafeteria and gave him a questioning look—they had planned to review for their chemistry test—but he nodded reassuringly. He'd make time for studying later.

"The prodigal son returns!" Akeem announced dramatically as Bear sat down. "What's the occasion?"

"Just wanted to hang with you guys," Bear said simply. "Talk about something other than football or school for a change."

For the next thirty minutes, Bear focused on being fully present—laughing at jokes, joining conversations, reconnecting with friends he'd been seeing but not really engaging with. By the end of lunch, he felt more relaxed than he had in weeks.

When the bell rang, he caught up with Heather in the hallway.

"Sorry about missing our study session," he said.

"It's okay," she assured him. "You looked like you were having fun with your friends."

"I was," Bear admitted. "I've been so focused on improvement that I've been neglecting relationships. But I still want to study for the test. Could we meet after practice?"

Heather hesitated. "I have to babysit my little brother after school."

"I could come to your house," Bear suggested. "If that's okay with your parents. We could study, and I could help with your brother too."

Heather looked surprised by the offer. "Really? He's nine and very energetic."

"Sounds like fun," Bear said genuinely. "I'm an only child. Always wanted a little brother to throw a football with."

That evening, Bear found himself sitting at the Chen family's kitchen table, alternating between balancing chemical equations with Heather and showing her brother Michael how to throw a perfect spiral in the backyard.

"You're good with him," Heather observed as they watched Michael practicing his newfound throwing technique. "Most people get annoyed by his energy."

"He's a great kid," Bear said. "Reminds me of myself at that age—always moving, always curious."

When Mrs. Chen arrived home from her job at the community college, she insisted Bear stay for dinner. As they ate, Bear found himself engaged in a lively discussion about everything from college football to the best fishing spots in the county.

"You should come over more often," Mr. Chen told Bear as he was leaving. "Michael hasn't stopped talking about football since you arrived."

"I'd like that," Bear replied, surprised to realize how much he meant it.

The next day, Bear approached Akeem after practice.

"Hey, I need your help with something."

"What's up?" Akeem asked, toweling off his face.

"I want to organize some extra passing sessions, but not just for me," Bear explained. "I was thinking we could invite some of the younger receivers, help them work on their routes and timing."

Akeem raised an eyebrow. "That's . . . actually a good idea. The freshman class has some talent, but they're raw."

"Exactly," Bear agreed. "And it's not just about making them better—it's about building connections across the team. Creating an environment where everyone elevates everyone else."

"Look at you, all philosophical," Akeem teased, but Bear could tell he was intrigued. "When do you want to start?"

"How about Thursday after practice? We could make it a weekly thing."

Akeem nodded. "I'm in. And I'll talk to Jenkins and Rodriguez; they might want to join too."

The first session exceeded Bear's expectations. Six receivers showed up, including three freshmen who normally wouldn't get much time with the varsity quarterbacks. Bear found himself naturally shifting into a teaching role, breaking down concepts and techniques in simple terms, just as Heather had done for him with chemistry.

"You're really good at this," one of the freshman receivers, Marcus, told him after successfully executing a post route they'd been working on. "Coach yells so much I can't always understand what he wants."

"Different people learn differently," Bear explained. "Sometimes you need to hear it, sometimes you need to see it, sometimes you need to do it repeatedly until it clicks."

As the session wrapped up, Coach Turner appeared on the sideline. He'd been watching from his office window.

"Good work out there, Wilson," he said. "What prompted you to take these young guys under your wing?"

"Just trying to build a stronger team, Coach," Bear replied.

Coach smiled approvingly, saying, "That's what leaders do."

On Saturday, Bear showed up at Tyler's house for the video game tournament, bringing chips and sodas because his mother had insisted he not arrive empty-handed. He was surprised to find not just football players but a mix of students from different social circles.

"Didn't know you were friends with the debate team," Bear remarked to Tyler as they set up the console.

Tyler shrugged. "My cousin's on the team. They're cool once you get to know them."

The afternoon turned into a marathon of competitive gaming, trash talk, and genuine camaraderie. Bear found himself enjoying the simple pleasure of spending time with peers without the pressure of performance or improvement.

"You're actually pretty good at this," Tyler commented after Bear eliminated him in the semifinals. "I thought you'd be rusty with all your studying and extra practices."

"Just because I'm serious about improvement doesn't mean I can't have fun," Bear replied with a grin. "Besides, gaming helps with reaction time and decision-making."

Tyler laughed. "Of course you'd find a way to make video games productive."

Later, as people were starting to leave, Tyler pulled Bear aside. "Hey, those passing sessions you're doing with the younger receivers—that's a good idea."

"Thanks," Bear said. "You're welcome to join if you want."

Tyler considered this. "Maybe I will."

Bear nodded, recognizing the olive branch for what it was. Their competition for the starting position was still real, but it didn't have to be antagonistic. They could push each other to be better while still working toward the common goal of team success.

The following week brought a new balance to Bear's life. He still studied diligently with Heather, trained intensely with Tony, and gave his all at team practices. But he also made time for relationships—eating lunch with his teammates some days, helping Heather's brother with his homework, organizing passing sessions that included players from all levels of the program.

During his next session with Tony, Bear shared what he'd been learning about balance and its importance.

"It's like going that extra inch to touch the line in relationships requires a different kind of discipline," Bear observed. "Not pushing harder, but being more present. Not doing more, but being more intentional with what I do."

Tony nodded approvingly. "That's wisdom, Bear. Excellence isn't about being one-dimensional. It's about being your best self in all dimensions of life."

"But how do you maintain that level of balance consistently?" Bear asked. "There are only so many hours in a day."

"It's not about perfect balance all the time," Tony clarified. "It's about rhythm—seasons of intensity followed by seasons

THE KEY IS INTENTIONALITY—CHOOSING YOUR EMPHASIS RATHER THAN LETTING CIRCUMSTANCES CHOOSE FOR YOU.

of recovery, seasons of focus followed by seasons of broader engagement. The key is *intentionality*—choosing your emphasis rather than letting circumstances choose for you."

He picked up a football. "Think of it like a quarterback's progression. You have primary targets, secondary options, check-downs. You don't force the ball to your first read if it's covered. You go through your progression, finding the best option for that specific situation."

Bear nodded, understanding the analogy. "So right now, football and academics might be my primary reads, but I still need to scan the field, stay aware of other options, other aspects of life."

"Exactly," Tony confirmed. "And sometimes, the best play is to check down to a relationship, a hobby, a moment of rest. Not because they're less important, but because they're what's open in that moment."

Over the next few weeks, Bear worked on implementing this more balanced approach. He still maintained his commitment to excellence in football and academics, but he also made space for other priorities:

- Sunday afternoons became protected family time, with no studying or film review allowed.
- Once a week, he and Heather spent their study session talking about non-academic interests.
- He joined a group text with friends who weren't on the football team, keeping those connections alive.
- He started leaving his phone in another room during dinner, giving his parents his full attention.

In his journal, Bear tracked these adjustments:

Today's Game: Building a life of balanced excellence

My Competition: The tendency to make football and academics my entire identity

Why It Matters: Because true excellence includes how we engage with all aspects of life

Going the extra inch doesn't always look like adding more—sometimes it looks like setting boundaries, creating space, being fully present in non-achievement con-

texts. The one-degree difference can be about intensity of focus, but it can also be about quality of presence.

As the season opener approached, the team's energy shifted. Two-a-days would end next Monday, and the season opener against Riverside was just three weeks away.

"You're practicing better than you have all spring and summer, Bear," Coach Turner observed after a particularly sharp practice. "Just as focused, but you seem more relaxed. What's changed?"

Bear considered the question before answering. "I've been working on balance, Coach. Making sure football stays my top priority but doesn't crowd out everything else in my life."

Coach nodded. "The best athletes I've coached have always had that balance—something else they care about besides their sport. Keeps them grounded, gives them perspective."

When he got home that night, Bear turned to his journal one more time:

I'm beginning to understand that the greatest excellence isn't found in single-minded pursuit of one goal at the expense of everything else. It's found in the balanced development of all my capacities—athletic, intellectual, relational, spiritual.

Maybe touching the line is as much about boundaries as it is about effort—knowing when to push and when to rest, when to focus and when to expand, when to strive and when to simply be.

I'm starting to think that the most challenging line to touch is the extra inch that separates a life of achievement from a life of meaning.

The next three weeks passed in a blur of final preparations. School, team meetings, film study, and last-minute adjustments to the playbook. Through it all, Bear maintained his newfound balance, giving his best to football while still making time for family dinners, study sessions with Heather, and occasional hangouts with friends.

Before he knew it, the countdown clock in the locker room showed just twenty-four hours until kickoff against Riverside. Tomorrow night, all their preparation would be put to the test.

THE COMPETE FRAMEWORK

C - CLARIFY THE GAME

O - OBSERVE THE RULES

M - MODEL WORLD-CLASS EXCELLENCE

P - OWN YOUR POSITION

E - EXECUTE TODAY

T - TAKE TIME

E - ENVIRONMENT

CHAPTER 8
OPENING NIGHT

There's nothing like the season opener in Texas high school football.

After weeks of anticipation, that long-awaited Friday night finally arrived. The lights of Jackson Creek Stadium blazed against the darkening Texas sky as Bear stood on the sideline, helmet in hand, watching the team warm up for the season opener against Riverside High. The stands were packed, the band was playing, and the energy was electric.

Bear scanned the crowd, spotting his parents in their usual seats near the 40-yard line. His father wore his old letter jacket despite the lingering summer heat, just as he did for every home game. A few rows behind them, Bear was surprised to see Tony, chatting with some other alumni.

In the locker room earlier, Coach Turner had delivered his pregame speech with characteristic intensity. "Everything we've done since January—every sprint, every rep in the weight room, every drill—has been preparation for tonight. But remember, preparation only creates opportunity. You still have to execute when it matters."

His eyes had moved deliberately across the room, meeting each player's gaze. Bear had nodded with every word Coach said, but he was disappointed inside. After all the work he'd put in over the summer, after all the growth and improvement, he was still the backup. The extra inch difference hadn't been enough—at least not yet.

Now, as the captains headed to midfield for the coin toss, Bear felt a mix of emotions. Part of him still burned to be the starter, to lead the team from the first snap. But another part—the part that had been learning from Tony all summer—recognized that this moment wasn't about his position on the depth chart. It was about how he responded to it.

Clarify what game you're playing, he reminded himself. *This isn't just about being the starter. It's about being excellent in whatever role you have. Be ready. Be supportive. Be a great teammate.*

"You good?" Akeem asked, noticing Bear's intense expression.

"Yeah," Bear replied, his focus sharpening. "Just getting my mind right."

"Greene's got this," Akeem assured him, misinterpreting Bear's concern. "But stay ready. You never know."

Bear nodded, appreciating the encouragement but realizing Akeem still saw the situation in the old way—as if Bear's only value was as an insurance policy against Tyler getting hurt or playing poorly.

But Bear's perspective had evolved. He wasn't just waiting for Tyler to fail. He was preparing to contribute, to excel in whatever opportunity came his way, to elevate his teammates whether he was on the field or not.

The game started well enough. Tyler led the offense on a scoring drive to open the game, connecting with Akeem for a 25-yard touchdown pass. The defense held Riverside to a field goal, and Jackson Creek led 7-3 at the end of the first quarter.

On the sideline, Bear wasn't just watching passively. He was studying the Riverside defense, noticing patterns, identifying vulnerabilities. When Tyler came off the field between series, Bear shared his observations.

"Their strong safety is cheating up on every first down," Bear pointed out. "If we show run and then go over the top, he's not going to be able to recover."

Tyler considered this, then nodded. "Good eye. I'll watch for that."

In the second quarter, Tyler threw an interception that Riverside returned for a touchdown. On the next drive, he seemed rattled, missing open receivers and taking an unnecessary sack. By halftime, Jackson Creek trailed 17-10.

In the locker room, Coach Turner addressed the team calmly but firmly. "We're beating ourselves out there. Too many mental errors, too many missed assignments. We need to refocus."

He turned to Tyler. "Greene, settle down. You're trying to force plays that aren't there. Trust the system."

Tyler nodded, but Bear could see the frustration in his eyes. The pressure of being the starting quarterback in a football-obsessed town was immense, especially for the season opener.

As the team prepared to return to the field, Bear approached Tyler. "Hey, you're doing fine. That interception wasn't on you—receiver ran the wrong route. Just play your game."

Tyler looked surprised by the encouragement, but managed a small smile. "Thanks."

The third quarter was a disaster. Tyler threw another interception, fumbled a snap, and seemed to be growing more frustrated with each mistake. The offense couldn't stay on the field, and the defense was wearing down from too much playing time. With 2 minutes left in the third quarter, Riverside led 31-10.

After a three-and-out where Tyler missed an open receiver on third down, Coach Turner called Bear over.

"Wilson, you're going in. Nothing fancy. Just execute the offense and give us a chance to get back in this game."

Bear's heart raced as he put on his helmet and jogged onto the field. This was the opportunity he'd been working for—though not how he'd imagined it would come.

As he approached the huddle, Bear saw the discouragement in his teammates' eyes. They were down by 3 touchdowns in the second half of their home opener. The energy that had filled the stadium at kickoff had largely dissipated.

But Bear had been preparing for this moment all summer. Not just physically but mentally. He'd visualized it, rehearsed it, and internalized the mindset needed to perform when opportunity came.

"One play at a time," he said calmly as he entered the huddle. "That's all we can control. Let's just win the next play."

The call was a simple 5-yard out to Akeem. As Bear settled under center, he focused on his breathing, slowing the game down mentally. The defense was showing blitz. Bear recognized it from film study—the same look Riverside had shown before bringing pressure off the edge earlier in the game.

"Lucky! Lucky!" Bear called, signaling a protection adjustment. The offensive line shifted, picking up the blitz perfectly when it came. Bear hit Akeem with a crisp throw, right on time, and the receiver turned upfield for a first down.

The next play was a screen pass to the running back for 8 yards. Bear was playing efficiently, taking what the defense gave him rather than trying to make the big play right away.

On third-and-2, he checked to a run at the line, and the running back picked up the first down. Suddenly, the offense was moving methodically down the field.

At the Riverside 30-yard line, Bear saw the safety cheating up—exactly the tendency he'd noticed earlier. He changed the play to a deep post. He stepped up in the pocket, set his feet, and delivered a perfect throw that hit the receiver in stride for a touchdown.

The Jackson Creek sideline erupted. It was still Riverside 31-17, but for the first time since the opening drive, there was energy and hope.

The defense, rejuvenated by the score, forced a quick three-and-out. When Bear got the ball back, he led another scoring drive, this one ending with a touchdown pass to Akeem on a well-executed fade route.

It was now 31-24, with 8 minutes left in the game.

Riverside tried to run the clock down, but Jackson Creek's defense forced another punt. Bear got the ball at his own 35-yard line with just under 4 minutes to play.

This was the moment. This was why he'd spent countless hours working on his mechanics, studying film, and yes, touching the line when no one was watching.

In the huddle, Bear looked at his teammates, now fully engaged and believing. "We've prepared for this. Trust your training. Trust each other. Win one play at a time."

He managed the drive with a veteran poise first-time players rarely exhibit, mixing quick passes with occasional runs to keep the defense honest. With each completion, each first down, the stadium grew louder, the energy building to a crescendo.

With 45 seconds left, Jackson Creek faced third-and-goal from the Riverside 8-yard line, trailing by 7.

Coach Turner called timeout and summoned Bear to the sideline. "You've got two plays to get this in. What do you like here?"

Bear thought for a moment, remembering the defensive tendencies he'd observed. "QB draw," he said confidently. "They're dropping eight into coverage. I can get this."

Coach nodded. "Do it. But if it's not there, get down, and we'll regroup on fourth down."

Back on the field, Bear called the play, took the snap, and feigned looking downfield before tucking the ball and darting up the middle. The linebackers, expecting pass, were too deep to stop him before he lunged into the end zone.

It was now 31-30. One extra point to tie, or go for 2 and the win?

Coach Turner didn't hesitate. He held up two fingers, signaling the offense to stay on the field. The home crowd roared its approval.

In the huddle, Bear looked at his teammates, now fully engaged and believing. "Sprint right option," he called. "Akeem, you're the primary read. Everyone else, sell your routes."

At the line, Bear surveyed the defense, looking for weaknesses. He took the snap, rolled right, and saw two defenders converge on Akeem. The tight end, running a shallow cross, was wide open.

Bear hit him in stride, and the tight end barreled into the end zone for the successful 2-point conversion. Jackson Creek 32, Riverside 31.

Riverside had one last desperate drive, but the Jackson Creek defense held firm. When the final whistle blew, the team stormed the field, celebrating an improbable comeback victory.

In the locker room afterward, Coach Turner addressed the team. "That's Jackson Creek football—never giving up, believing in each other, executing when it matters most."

He paused.

"Wilson, way to step up tonight. You showed great leadership out there."

He turned to Tyler. "Greene, this doesn't change anything immediately. You're still our starter. But this is a team, and everyone has to earn their spot every day. That's how we get better."

As the team dispersed, Tyler approached Bear by his locker. There was an awkward moment of tension before Tyler extended his hand. "Good game, Wilson. You earned that."

Bear shook his hand. "Thanks. We won as a team."

"Yeah, but you were the spark," Tyler acknowledged. Then, lowering his voice, he added, "What you did tonight—that's what this whole 'touching the line' thing you've been talking about looks like, isn't it?"

Bear looked at him in surprise. "How did you—"

"Tony Brewer's been talking to me too," Tyler admitted. "Started right after that conditioning workout where Coach called me out for not touching the line. Tony saw it and offered to help me understand what I was missing."

Bear absorbed this information, realizing that Tony had been mentoring not just him but Tyler as well. Instead of feeling betrayed, he felt a strange sense of respect for both of them.

"So you've been working the COMPETE framework too?" Bear asked.

Tyler nodded. "And TODAY. It's changing how I approach everything, not just football." He hesitated. "I always thought my talent would be enough. But Tony helped me see that talent without discipline is wasted potential."

TALENT WITHOUT DISCIPLINE IS WASTED POTENTIAL.

Before Bear could respond, his parents arrived to congratulate him, and the conversation with Tyler ended. But as Bear celebrated with his family, he caught Tony's eye across the locker room. Tony gave him a subtle nod of approval that meant more to Bear than all the touchdowns in the world.

Later that night, after a celebratory dinner with his parents, Bear took a moment alone in his room before bed. The adrenaline had finally worn off, leaving him physically exhausted but mentally clear.

He opened his journal, thinking about everything that had happened—not just tonight, but throughout the summer and fall. His journey from frustrated backup to tonight's comeback hero had been more complex than simply improving his football skills.

Today's Game: Stepping up when my moment came

My Competition: The pressure of the situation and the voice that said "don't mess up"

Why It Matters: Because touching the line in practice prepared me to perform when it counted

This isn't just about me versus Tyler anymore. It's about all of us getting better together. Maybe that's the biggest lesson of all.

The one-degree difference showed up tonight. Not just in completions or touchdowns, but in preparation, in mindset, in leadership. When opportunity met preparation, the water became ice.

Bear closed the journal, a sense of peaceful satisfaction settling over him. Tonight's game had been a validation of everything he'd been working toward. Not just the victory or his individual performance, but the way he'd led, the way he'd connected with his teammates, the way he'd executed under pressure.

Yet even as he savored the moment, Bear knew this was just one game. Tyler was the still the starter. And Bear's real test would be what came next—how he handled success, how he maintained his discipline when praise was flowing, how he continued to touch the line even when everyone was watching.

As he drifted off to sleep, Bear found himself thinking not about the touchdowns, but about the look in his teammates' eyes when they started to believe that the game wasn't over and they could come back to win. That, he realized, was what mattered most—the power to lift others, to create something greater than the sum of its parts.

And that power came from the same place as individual excellence: from the discipline to go that one extra inch to touch the line when no one was watching.

The next morning, Bear awoke to a text message from Tony: *Well done. But remember, success is a far more challenging test of character than failure. The real work begins now.*

Bear smiled, recognizing the truth in Tony's words. Last night had been exhilarating, but it was just one step in a longer journey. The principles that had gotten him here—clarifying what game he was playing, observing the rules of excellence, modeling the best, positioning himself honestly, executing with purpose, taking time to reflect, and choosing his environment—would be even more important now.

CHAPTER 9

THE TEAM DIVIDE

Bear walked into school that Monday after the season opener expecting things to be different. And they were, but not in the way he'd anticipated. Instead of united celebration over their comeback victory, he found himself caught in an uncomfortable situation.

Some teammates—especially those who played offense—were treating him like the team's savior, suggesting openly that he should be the starter. Others, particularly Tyler's closer friends, were defensive and dismissive of Bear's performance, insisting it was just one good quarter against a tired defense.

By lunchtime, the team was showing subtle but concerning signs of division. In the cafeteria, Bear noticed players choosing sides by where they sat—those who supported him at one table, those loyal to Tyler at another.

"You're the real QB1," one of the receivers said as Bear sat down with his lunch tray. "Everyone knows it now."

Bear frowned. "That's not how it works. Coach decides the depth chart, not popular opinion."

"Yeah, but after Friday—"

"After Friday, we're 1-0 as a team," Bear interrupted firmly. "That's what matters."

He glanced across the cafeteria where Tyler sat with another group of players. Their eyes met briefly before Tyler looked away.

This wasn't what Bear wanted. Yes, he wanted to be the starter, but not like this—not at the cost of team unity.

During his study period, Bear checked his phone and saw several social media notifications. Curious, he opened up the local sports page's account and saw they'd posted about his performance on Friday, with comments debating whether he should replace Tyler as the starter.

Even worse, several of his teammates had posted about the "quarterback controversy," taking sides publicly. Some of the comments were downright nasty, attacking either him or Tyler.

Bear felt a knot forming in his stomach. The team was dividing into factions, and he was at the center of it. How could he navigate this situation without making things worse? How could he lead by example when he was still figuring things out himself?

This wasn't just team division anymore—it was playing out for the whole community to see. And he knew from experience how toxic social media could become, how it could amplify divisions and create false narratives.

He texted Tony: *Need advice. Team dividing into "Team Bear" and "Team Tyler" on social media. Getting ugly.*

Tony responded quickly: *Meet me at the library after school before practice. Bring Tyler if you can.*

Bear hesitated, then texted Tyler: *Can we talk before practice? Library at 3 p.m. Important.*

To his surprise, Tyler replied: *Okay.*

After school, Bear found Tyler already waiting in a quiet corner of the library. His expression was guarded.

"Thanks for coming," Bear said, sitting down across from him.

"What's this about?" Tyler asked, though his tone suggested he already knew.

"The team division. The social media stuff. It's getting out of hand."

Tyler nodded grimly. "Tell me about it. My own cousin posted that I should be benched."

Bear winced and said, "That's rough."

"It's not your fault," Tyler acknowledged.

Before Bear could respond, Tony appeared, pulling up a chair to join them. "Glad you're both here. We need to talk about comparison—the healthy kind and the toxic kind."

He placed his phone, open to one of the social media discussions about the quarterback situation, on the table. "This right here is toxic comparison. It pits you against each other, creates false narratives, and divides what should be united." Tyler and Bear both nodded, understanding his point.

"Social media has made this worse," Tony continued. "It's constant, it's public, and it creates the illusion that we must always be measuring ourselves against others. That our worth comes from being 'better than' someone else."

"So what do we do?" Bear asked. "We can't control what other people post."

"No, but you can control how you respond and what you model," Tony replied. "The first step is recognizing when you're falling into the quicksand of negative comparison."

"How do you know?" Tyler asked.

"When comparison makes you feel inadequate, resentful, or superior—that's the bad kind," Tony explained. "When it inspires you to improve or helps you learn from others—that's the good kind."

He turned to Bear. "When you first started comparing yourself to Tyler, how did it make you feel?"

Bear thought back to the beginning of the season. "Inadequate. Like I could never match his natural talent."

"And now?"

"Now I see how watching him can help me improve certain aspects of my game. And I recognize that we bring different strengths to the team."

Tony nodded his approval, then turned to Tyler. "And you? How has comparing yourself to Bear affected you?"

Tyler considered this. "At first, I didn't really compare myself to him at all. I was the starter, period." He paused. "But when I saw his work ethic, his discipline . . . it challenged me. Made me realize I was coasting at times."

"That's the difference," Tony said. "Unhealthy comparison focuses on outcomes—who's the starter, who gets the glory, who's 'better.' Healthy comparison focuses on process—what

I can learn, how I can improve, how we can make each other better."

He leaned back in his chair. "Here's a strategy I want you both to try. Whenever you notice yourself making a comparison, ask three questions: Is this making me better? Is this within my control? Is this about growth or about ego?"

Bear and Tyler both nodded, taking this in.

"Now," Tony continued, "about the team division. You two need to model healthy competition—what it looks like to compete with each other rather than against each other."

"How do we do that?" Bear asked.

"By being publicly united," Tony answered. "By supporting each other visibly. By making it clear to everyone that you're focused on team success, not individual glory."

Tyler nodded slowly. "We need to shut down the 'Team Tyler' versus 'Team Bear' narrative."

"Exactly," Tony confirmed. "And it starts with you two setting the example."

After Tony left, Tyler and Bear remained in the library, strategizing how to address the division on the team.

"What if we posted something together?" Bear suggested. "Show everyone we're on the same page."

Tyler considered this. "That could work. But actions speak louder than words. We need to demonstrate being on the same page at practice, too."

By the time they walked to the locker room to prepare for practice, they had a plan. As the team was getting ready, Tyler called for everyone's attention.

"Listen up," he said. "I've seen the comments online. People trying to create division between me and Wilson, between different groups on this team. It stops now."

He looked at Bear, who stepped forward.

"We're one team," Bear emphasized. "There's not a 'Team Tyler' or a 'Team Bear.' There's only one team that matters—the Panthers."

Tyler nodded. "What happened Friday wasn't about one player saving the day. It was about all of us executing when it mattered. And that's what we'll continue to do, whoever is taking the snaps."

The message was clear, and the team responded. At practice that day, the tension had noticeably decreased. When Tyler made a good throw, Bear was the first to acknowledge it. When Bear missed a read during his reps, Tyler pulled him aside to point out what he'd seen from the defense.

After practice, in the locker room, Bear opened Instagram and saw a notification. Tyler had posted a photo of the two of them from practice, with the caption, "Iron sharpens iron." His message read, *Competing with my brother @BearWilsonQB every day to make us both better. #OnePantherNation.*

Bear smiled and immediately shared it to his own profile, adding: *When we compete against each other, we both lose. When we compete with each other, the entire team wins. Grateful for a teammate who makes me better every day. #CompeteEveryDay.*

The posts quickly gathered likes and supportive comments, shifting the narrative from division to unity. By evening, several other teammates had shared similar messages of team solidarity.

When Bear got home, he found his parents in the kitchen preparing dinner together. "How was practice?" his father asked.

"Good," Bear replied. "Actually, better than good. Tyler and I are working on bringing the team together, stopping this 'quarterback controversy' stuff before it gets worse."

His mother looked up from chopping vegetables. "That's mature of both of you. It would be easy to get caught up in you versus him."

"I've been on both sides of that situation," his father added. "When I played, there was always competition for positions. The teams that succeeded were the ones where teammates made each other better instead of tearing each other down."

Bear nodded. "That's exactly what Tony talked about today—healthy versus unhealthy comparison."

"Tony Brewer's turning out to be quite the mentor," his mother observed. "Teaching you about a lot more than just football mechanics."

"Yeah," Bear agreed. "He had us ask three questions whenever we find ourselves comparing: Is this making me better? Is this within my control? Is this about growth or about ego?"

His father nodded approvingly. "Smart questions. Wish I'd had someone teaching me that at your age."

Bear continued. "I'm starting to see how social media creates all these unhealthy comparisons in every area of life. People posting only their highlights, making everyone else feel inadequate."

"The highlight reel versus the behind-the-scenes reality," his mother agreed. "I see it with my students all the time.

They're comparing their whole lives to someone else's perfectly curated snapshot."

The next day at school, the atmosphere had shifted noticeably. The divided lunch tables were gone, with offensive and defensive players mixing again.

During chemistry, Heather passed Bear a note: *Saw your post with Tyler. That was really cool.*

Bear scribbled back: *Learning that excellence includes how you handle relationships, not just how you perform.*

At lunch, Akeem slid onto the bench across from Bear. "So, you and Tyler are besties now?" he asked with a hint of sarcasm.

"Not exactly," Bear replied. "We're just recognizing that we can push each other to be better without dividing the team."

"Well, whatever you're doing seems to be working," Akeem said. "Practice yesterday was the best vibe we've had all season."

Bear nodded, noticing that Tyler had just entered the cafeteria. He caught Tyler's eye and motioned him over to their table—a simple gesture, but one that spoke volumes.

For a moment, Tyler hesitated, then changed direction to join them. A few of his usual lunch companions looked confused, then followed him.

"Making room for everyone?" Tyler asked as he set down his tray.

"That's the idea," Bear confirmed.

As lunch continued, the conversation flowed naturally—about the upcoming game, classes, weekend plans. It wasn't forced camaraderie but genuine interaction. The division that had been forming was starting to heal.

After school, Coach Turner called Bear and Tyler into his office before practice.

"I noticed what you two did yesterday," he said without preamble. "The way you addressed the team, the social media posts, how you worked together in practice."

Bear and Tyler exchanged a glance.

"That's leadership," Coach continued. "Putting the team above yourselves. I've coached for twenty years, and I can tell you this: Talent may win games, but teamwork wins championships."

TALENT MAY WIN GAMES, BUT TEAMWORK WINS CHAMPIONSHIPS.

He leaned forward. "Here's what we're going to do moving forward. Greene, you're still our starter. You've earned that over the past year. But Wilson, you're going to get specific packages designed for your skill set. Both of you will play, both of you will lead, both of you will make the team better."

Neither quarterback objected. It was a solution that recognized Tyler's seniority and experience while also acknowledging Bear's growth and contribution.

"One more thing," Coach added. "I want you two to run a quarterback meeting every Thursday—break down film together, work with the receivers, develop your timing. Show everyone what healthy competition looks like."

As they left the coach's office, Tyler said, "That's actually a good idea. The quarterback meeting."

"Yeah," Bear agreed. "We see different things on film. Together we might catch twice as much."

"And the packages for you make sense," Tyler added, surprising Bear with his acceptance. "You've earned playing time. And honestly, it keeps me from getting complacent."

Before they parted ways to change for practice, Tyler added, "You know, when I first saw all those posts about how you should replace me, I was pretty angry. Not at you, but at the situation."

"I would have felt the same way," Bear admitted.

"But then I thought about what Tony's been teaching me," Tyler continued. "About clarifying what game I'm really playing. And I realized: If my goal is just to protect my starting position, I'm thinking too small. But if my goal is to be the best quarterback I can be, to lead this team to a championship, then having you push me actually helps."

Bear nodded, understanding completely. "Iron sharpens iron."

"Exactly," Tyler said with a small smile. "See you on the field."

That Thursday, Bear and Tyler held their first quarterback meeting. They invited not just the varsity receivers but the JV and freshman quarterbacks as well, creating a learning environment that spanned the program. They broke down film together, showing how they each read defenses, made adjustments, and processed information. The younger quarterbacks were particularly engaged, seeing up close how two different styles—Tyler's natural arm talent and improvisational ability,

Bear's methodical approach and disciplined mechanics—could both be effective.

"You guys should do this every week," Marcus, one of the freshman receivers, said as they wrapped up. "This is better than regular practice."

Bear and Tyler exchanged a look of satisfaction. They were creating something valuable, not just for themselves, but for the whole program.

In his journal that night, Bear reflected on everything that had happened since the season opener:

Today's Game: Building team unity despite competition for the same position

My Competition: The temptation to let social media comparison divide rather than unite

Why It Matters: Because a divided team has a lower ceiling than a united one

I'm learning that comparison isn't inherently bad—it's how we use it that matters. When it becomes about ego or status, it divides. When it's about growth and improvement, it unites. The small decision to work with Tyler instead of against him might change the entire season.

Strategies for healthy comparison:

1. *Is this making me better?*
2. *Is this within my control?*
3. *Is this about growth or about ego?*

When I focus on these questions, the path becomes clear. The real competition isn't Bear vs. Tyler. It's Me vs. Me.

As Bear closed his journal, he felt a deep sense of satisfaction. The team was stronger than it had been a week ago. He and Tyler were pushing each other to improve while also elevating everyone around them. And he was seeing firsthand how the principles Tony had taught him—about going that extra inch to touch the line, about the one-degree difference, about healthy competition—applied far beyond football.

The quarterback controversy hadn't disappeared entirely. In a small town like Jackson Creek, coffee shops and sports columns still voiced their opinions about who should start. But those opinions no longer came from within the locker room or threatened to divide the team, because the two players at the center of the controversy refused to be divided.

Sometimes the most important line to touch wasn't on a football field or in a classroom. Sometimes it was the extra inch between ego and character, between self-interest and team success, between unhealthy comparison and mutual growth.

That was the line Bear committed to touch every day so he could elevate not only himself but also everyone around him.

As September turned to October and the Panthers continued their winning streak, Bear began to wonder: where had these principles come from originally? His parents had taught him values of hard work and integrity since childhood, but he'd never heard them articulate concepts like "touching the line" or "the one-degree difference" specifically.

Tony clearly lived by these principles, but where had he learned them? Did they originate with him, or had they been passed down from someone else? And if the latter, how far back did this chain of wisdom extend?

These questions lingered in Bear's mind as he headed home Friday night after another victory, curious about the foundations that had supported his recent growth.

CHAPTER 10

FAMILY FOUNDATIONS

September gave way to October, bringing crisp mornings and a new rhythm to Bear's life. The Panthers had compiled a 3-1 record through the first month of the season, with their two-quarterback system evolving from awkward experiment to strategic advantage.

"Bear! Breakfast!"

His mother's voice drifted up the stairs, pulling Bear from the playbook he'd been studying since dawn. While most of his friends were still sleeping off Friday night's victory over Central High, Saturday mornings meant meeting Coach Gideon at the field house to grade film from the night before. Bear had been up since six, making notes before he and Tyler had to start the film session.

"Coming!" he called back, grabbing his playbook and shoes before heading downstairs.

The kitchen was filled with the familiar weekend scents of bacon, coffee, and his mother's blueberry pancakes. His father sat at the table, newspaper spread out before him, reading glasses perched on the end of his nose.

"Morning, son," Robert Wilson said, looking up with a smile. "Productive study session?"

Bear nodded, sliding into his usual seat. "Central's defense has some tendencies I'm picking up on. Might be useful for the rematch if we see them in the playoffs."

His father folded the paper, giving Bear his full attention. "You're thinking ahead. Good."

Ellen Wilson placed a stack of pancakes in front of Bear. "Eat first, think about football second. You've been at it since sunrise."

Bear smiled at his mother's familiar concern. "Thanks, Mom."

As they ate, the conversation flowed easily, touching on the previous night's game, his father's store, his mother's upcoming parent-teacher conferences. This was their rhythm—comfortable, supportive, grounded in the everyday details that formed the backbone of family life.

"So," his mother said as she refilled his orange juice, "how are things going with all your . . . frameworks? The ones Tony's been teaching you."

Bear paused, fork halfway to his mouth. It wasn't that his parents didn't know about his work with Tony—he'd shared much of it with them. But his mother's tone suggested she was asking something deeper.

"Good," he replied. "They're helping me see things differently. Not just in football, but in everything."

"Like what?" his father prompted.

Bear considered the question. "Like understanding that excellence isn't just about outcomes—it's about the process, the small choices that build up over time. And how comparing yourself to others can be toxic unless you use it the right way."

His mother nodded thoughtfully. "I've noticed a change in you these past few months. You've always been driven, but now there's something else. A kind of . . . groundedness."

"That's a good way to put it," his father agreed. "You seem less anxious about results and more focused on your work instead."

Bear was surprised by their observations. He'd been so immersed in his own journey that he hadn't fully registered how visible the changes might be to others, especially those who knew him best.

"I guess I've been learning that trying to be the best version of myself is more important than trying to be a better version of someone else," he said.

"That's wisdom beyond your years," his mother said with a smile. "Took me until my thirties to figure that out."

His father leaned back in his chair. "You know, Bear, your mother and I have tried to teach you similar principles over the years. About hard work, integrity, doing things right even when no one's watching. But sometimes you need to hear those things from someone else for them to really sink in."

"It's not that I didn't hear you," Bear clarified, not wanting them to think he'd dismissed their guidance. "It's just . . . Tony put it in terms that connected with where I am right now."

"We understand," his mother assured him. "That's why we've been so supportive of your work with him. Every generation needs mentors who can bridge the gap between parental wisdom and real-world application."

After breakfast, Bear's father asked if he wanted to come to the auto parts store for a few hours after his film session with Coach Gideon. It was a familiar weekend routine, one that had been somewhat displaced by Bear's increasingly packed schedule.

"I'd like that," Bear said, realizing he'd missed this time with his father.

Wilson Auto Supply was a Jackson Creek institution, serving the community for over thirty years. Robert Wilson had started working there right out of high school, eventually buying it from the previous owner when Bear was just a toddler. It wasn't a large business, but it was successful, respected, and, in an era of big-box stores and online shopping, remarkably resilient.

Just before lunch, Bear pulled up to the store just as his dad was finishing up sweeping the front entrance. Bear followed along, helping as he had since he was old enough to stock shelves.

"How do you do it, Dad?" Bear asked. "Keep the store going when there's so much competition from the chains or the internet?"

His father considered this. "The easy answer is relationships. People know us, trust us. But that's not the whole story. The real answer is in the details—the things customers don't even consciously notice but that make all the difference.

"Watch this," his father said as a customer entered, a middle-aged man in work clothes. "Happy Saturday, Bill. How's that water pump working out?"

The man looked surprised, then pleased. "Great, Bob. Fixed the problem right away. Thanks for recommending that brand."

"Glad to hear it. What brings you in today?"

As the customer explained his need for a specific carburetor part, Bear watched his father listen attentively, asking clarifying questions, then walking directly to the exact shelf where the part was located.

"That's the one," the customer confirmed. "You always know your inventory."

"We try," Robert said modestly.

After the transaction was complete and the customer had left, Bear's father turned to him. "See what happened there?"

"You remembered what he bought before," Bear observed.

"Yes, but more than that. I remembered his name, his vehicle, his specific issue. Made him feel valued, like more than just a transaction." He straightened a display of oil filters. "That's the extra inch in business—the small details that competitors overlook but that build loyalty over time."

Throughout the day, Bear observed this pattern repeatedly. His father knew most customers by name, remembered their vehicles and repair histories, and often anticipated their needs before they fully articulated them.

During a lull in customers, Bear asked, "How do you keep all that information in your head? All the people, all the parts, all the problems?"

His father smiled. "I don't always. But I make a point to write down important details after interactions. A customer mentions his daughter just started college? I note that. Someone's rebuilding a classic car? I keep track of which parts they've bought and which they might need next."

He pulled a small notebook from his pocket. "This isn't just a record of transactions. It's a record of relationships."

Bear thought of his own journal, where he tracked his progress and reflections. "So you've been touching the line in business all along."

"That's a good way to put it," his father agreed. "In any field, the difference between good and great often comes down to these small details—the things most people can't be bothered with but that compound over time."

As the day progressed, Bear helped customers, restocked shelves, and observed his father in his element. It struck him that his dad embodied many of the principles Tony had been teaching:

Clarifying what game he was playing (personal service in an impersonal market)

Observing the rules of excellence (attention to detail, product knowledge)

Modeling the best (studying successful independents)

Positioning honestly (focusing on strengths rather than trying to compete on price alone)

Executing consistently

Taking time to reflect, review, and rest

and

creating an Environment of mutual respect and trust

"You know," Bear said as they ate lunch in the small break room, "I think you and Tony would have a lot to talk about. You approach business the same way he approaches football."

His father chuckled. "Well, excellence has common principles, whatever the field. Your mother is the same way with her teaching. Have you ever watched her grade papers?"

Bear shook his head. "Not really."

"You should sometime. The care she takes, the personal notes she writes to each student, the way she tailors her feedback to individual learning styles—it's remarkable."

Bear realized he'd never thought much about his mother's professional approach. He knew she was dedicated, often spending evenings and weekends grading or preparing lessons. But he'd never considered the specific ways she applied excellence to her teaching.

That evening, after dinner, Bear wandered into the den where his mother was grading essays at her desk. Stacks of papers surrounded her, along with colorful pens, sticky notes, and a mug of tea.

"Mind if I hang out?" he asked, settling into an armchair with his chemistry textbook.

"Not at all," she replied, smiling briefly before returning to her work.

For the next hour, Bear alternated between studying and observing his mother. He noticed she didn't just mark errors—she wrote extensive comments in the margins, asked thoughtful questions, suggested specific improvements. Each paper seemed to receive her complete attention, as if it were the only one rather than one of dozens.

"How do you maintain that level of focus?" Bear finally asked. "Doesn't it get boring after a while of reviewing the same paper over and over again, year after year?"

His mother looked up, seeming surprised by the question.

"Sometimes," she admitted. "But I try to remember that behind each paper is a student who deserves my best effort. Just as I expect their best effort on the assignment."

"That sounds like going the extra inch," Bear observed.

"Is that one of Tony's phrases?" she asked.

Bear nodded, explaining the concept—how the small choice to touch the line when tired or when no one is watching builds character and excellence over time.

"That's a powerful metaphor," his mother said. "And yes, I suppose that's what I'm trying to do. These comments might seem like small things, but to a student struggling with a concept or lacking confidence, those comments can make all the difference in how they see themselves."

She set down her pen. "You know, teaching is similar to quarterbacking in some ways. It's not just about knowing the material—it's about communication, about connection, about bringing out the best in others."

Bear had never considered the parallel, but now it seemed obvious. "You've been modeling leadership for me all along," he said, the realization suddenly dawning on him.

His mother smiled. "Your father and I both try to live what we believe, not just talk about it. That's the most important lesson we could teach you."

Later that night, as Bear prepared for bed, he found himself reflecting on the day's revelations. His parents had been quietly demonstrating the principles of excellence throughout his life—not through grand speeches or dramatic gestures, but through consistent, everyday choices.

His father's meticulous attention to customer details, his mother's thoughtful engagement with each student's work—these were manifestations of the same principles Tony had been teaching him. Touching the line. The one-degree difference. Excellence in the margins.

In his journal, Bear wrote:

Today's Game: Recognizing the foundations of excellence in my own family

My Competition: Taking for granted the examples right in front of me

Why It Matters: Because understanding where my values come from helps me live them more intentionally

I've been so focused on applying Tony's frameworks to football and school that I almost missed how my parents have been modeling these principles all along. Dad's commitment to knowing his customers as people, not just buyers. Mom's dedication to giving each student her full attention and best effort.

They've been showing me what excellence looks like in the small, everyday choices that most people overlook.

Bear closed his journal, feeling a deeper connection to his family and a greater appreciation for the values they had instilled in him. The principles Tony was teaching weren't foreign concepts after all—they were already woven into the fabric of his upbringing, just expressed in different ways.

And in that realization, Bear found a new layer of motivation. He wasn't just pursuing excellence for himself or to win a starting position. He was honoring a legacy of commitment to doing things right that had been passed down to him by his parents.

The next morning, as he prepared for his regular session with Tony, Bear felt a renewed sense of purpose. He was part of something larger than himself—a tradition of excellence that spanned generations and transcended any particular field or pursuit.

And in that tradition, the extra inch—the small, consistent choices that separated good from great—wasn't just a strategy for success.

It was a way of life.

IT WAS A WAY OF LIFE.

CHAPTER 11

PERSONAL COST

As October continued, the Jackson Creek Panthers maintained their momentum. Another win followed their victory over Central High, bringing their record to 4-1. The two-quarterback system with Tyler starting and Bear coming in for specific packages was working well; the offense was more diverse and unpredictable with both quarterbacks contributing.

More importantly, there were no signs of the team division that had threatened them after the season opener. Tyler and Bear's example of competing with each other rather than against each other had spread throughout the team. Players were pushing each other in practice, celebrating each other's successes, and holding each other accountable to higher standards.

Bear's life had fallen into a demanding but fulfilling routine: morning sessions with Tony, classes (including chemistry, where he was now maintaining a solid B average thanks to his continued study sessions with Heather), afternoon practice, film study, homework, sleep, and repeat. His journal entries became more focused on long-term growth than immediate results.

One Tuesday in mid-October, during their regular morning session, Tony brought up something Bear hadn't considered.

"You've been talking a lot about the team environment and how it's improved," Tony observed. "But what about your personal environment? The circle of people and influences outside of football?"

Bear thought about it. "What do you mean, exactly?"

"I mean, who do you spend most of your time with when you're not on the field? What influences are you allowing into your life? Are they lifting your ceiling or limiting it?"

ARE THEY LIFTING YOUR CEILING OR LIMITING IT?

Bear had to admit he hadn't given it much thought. His focus had been so narrow—football, classes, more football—that he'd hardly had time for anything else.

"I guess mostly the team," he answered. "And my parents. And Heather for chemistry. That's about it lately."

Tony nodded. "And what are you sacrificing for this schedule? What's the cost?"

The question caught Bear off guard. "Cost?"

"Everything has a cost," Tony explained. "Every choice to do one thing is a choice not to do something else. I'm not saying your choices are wrong . . . I'm just asking if you're conscious of what you're giving up."

Bear considered this. He'd turned down several social invitations in the past months. His old hobby of fishing with his dad had fallen by the wayside. Even family dinners had become rushed affairs as he hurried through meals to get back to studying playbooks or homework.

"I guess I've been pretty one-dimensional lately," Bear admitted. "But isn't that what it takes? To touch the line in everything, don't I have to be all in on what matters most?"

"There's a difference between being all in and being out of balance," Tony replied. "Remember the 'T' in TODAY—Timing: Master Your Season. Different seasons require different strategies."

He leaned forward. "Right now, you're in a growth season for football and academics. That's appropriate. But be careful not to sacrifice relationships and experiences that give your life meaning beyond those pursuits."

As Tony drove him home, Bear thought about this conversation. Was he becoming too narrowly focused? Was there a cost to his relentless pursuit of improvement that he wasn't acknowledging?

When he arrived home, he found his parents in the living room, his father reading a book and his mother grading papers.

"How was the session with Tony?" his mother asked, looking up with a smile.

"Good," Bear replied automatically. Then, after a moment's hesitation, he added, "Actually, it was different. Tony talked about balance, about what I might be sacrificing for football and school."

His father set down his book. "What do you think about that?"

Bear shrugged. "I don't know. I mean, excellence requires sacrifice, right? You can't be great at something without putting in the hours."

"That's true," his father acknowledged. "But there's a difference between necessary sacrifices and unnecessary ones. Some things you give up because you have to. Others you give up because you haven't figured out how to fit them in yet."

His mother nodded in agreement. "It's about prioritization, not elimination. The goal isn't to have only one or two things in your life—it's to give each thing its proper place and time."

Bear thought about this. "I guess I have been letting some things slide. Like our fishing trips," he added, looking at his father.

His father smiled. "I've missed those too, son."

"And I've been rushing through dinner to get back to studying," Bear admitted to his mother.

"We've noticed," she said gently. "We understand why, but we miss the conversations we used to have."

That night, in his room, Bear pulled out his journal and created a new entry:

Today's Game: Finding balance while pursuing excellence

My Competition: The belief that success requires total sacrifice of everything else

Why It Matters: Because a one-dimensional life, even an excellent one, is still incomplete

I've been so focused on touching the line in football and academics that I've neglected other areas—family time, friendships, hobbies, rest. Tony challenged me to think differently and showed me that excellence doesn't have to come at the cost of everything else. It's about strategic allocation of time and energy, not elimination of everything except the primary goal.

TODAY Check:

T—Recognize what season I'm in, but also what else needs attention.

O—Prioritize all important relationships, not just football ones.

D—Football is only a few more months; my friendships will go with me throughout life.

A—Choose a mindset of abundance, not scarcity, about time.

Y—Try to be better balanced today than I was yesterday.

The next morning, Bear woke up with a new resolve. He would maintain his commitment to excellence in football and academics, but he would also be more intentional about making space for other important aspects of life.

At breakfast, he asked his father, "Are you free this Saturday? Maybe we could go fishing after my film session if the weather's good."

His father looked up, surprised and pleased. "I'd like that. It's been too long."

"And Mom?" Bear added, "I was thinking we could have dinner together tonight without my rushing off to study. Maybe actually talk about something other than football or school."

His mother smiled. "I'd love that, Bear."

At school that day, Bear made a point of engaging with friends he'd been seeing but not really connecting with. During lunch, instead of immediately diving into chemistry notes with Heather, he asked about her weekend, her family, and her interests outside of academics.

"You're different today," Heather observed. "More . . . present."

Bear nodded. "I'm trying to be. I realized I've been so focused on goals and improvement that I've been missing what's right in front of me."

Heather smiled. "Well, I like it. Though we should probably still review the periodic table at some point."

"Definitely," Bear agreed. "But maybe we can also talk about normal stuff sometimes."

"Like what?" Heather asked, genuinely curious.

Bear hesitated, realizing he wasn't entirely sure what "normal teenage stuff" entailed anymore. "I don't know. Movies? Music? Whatever you're interested in besides chemistry."

"I play violin," Heather offered. "Been taking lessons since I was six."

"Really? I had no idea."

"You never asked," she pointed out gently.

Bear felt a twinge of guilt, recognizing the truth in her words. He'd been benefiting from Heather's help with chemistry for weeks, but had shown little interest in her life beyond that.

"Well, I'm asking now," he said. "Tell me about your violin playing."

As Heather talked about her music—her favorite pieces, the concerts she'd performed in, her dream of playing in a university orchestra someday—Bear realized how much richness he'd been missing by narrowing his focus so completely.

After school, during their quarterback meeting, Bear suggested to Tyler that they wrap up a bit earlier than usual.

"I've been thinking about what Coach said about team bonding," Bear explained. "Maybe we should organize something outside of football. Get to know each other as people, not just players."

Tyler considered this. "Like what?"

"I don't know. A cookout at someone's house? Fishing trip? Something where we can just hang out without footballs or playbooks."

"That's actually not a bad idea," Tyler admitted. "Team chemistry isn't just built on the field."

They floated the idea to the rest of the team, and the response was enthusiastic. They settled on a Saturday cookout at Akeem's house, whose parents had a large backyard with a pool.

That Saturday, Bear raced home from the film session to start the fishing trip with his father. The local lake was peaceful that afternoon.

"So," his father said as they settled in with their fishing rods, "how's the balancing act going?"

Bear smiled. "Better. I'm trying to be more intentional about making time for things besides football and school. It's not as easy as I thought it would be."

His father nodded. "Balance isn't about equal time for everything. It's about appropriate attention to what matters most in each season of life." He cast his line into the still water. "Right now, football and academics should be priorities. But not to the exclusion of everything—or everyone—else."

"That's basically what Tony said," Bear observed.

"Smart man," his father replied. "Took me years to learn that lesson. I almost lost your mother over it, back when I was first building the business."

Bear looked up in surprise. His parents' relationship had always seemed solid, unshakable. "Really?"

His father nodded, a wistful expression crossing his face. "I was working sixteen-hour days, seven days a week. Thought I was doing it for us, for our future. But I was missing the present—missing her, missing our life together."

"What happened?"

"She finally sat me down and said, 'Robert, I didn't marry you to be alone all the time.' Made me realize I was building a business at the cost of my marriage."

He reeled in his line and cast again. "That was my wake-up call. I started setting boundaries, hired help even though we could barely afford it, made sure we had dinner together almost every night."

Bear absorbed this, seeing his father in a new light. "How did you find the right balance?"

"Trial and error, mostly," his father admitted with a laugh. "But I learned to ask a simple question: Will this matter in five years? Some things will—graduating college, building a career, finding the right partner. Others won't—most daily work emergencies, small setbacks, temporary challenges."

They fished in silence for a while, each lost in their own thoughts. Bear caught one bass, his father caught two, and they released them all back into the lake.

"You know what I love about fishing?" his father said as they packed up their gear. "It forces you to slow down, to be patient, to appreciate the moment. Can't rush the fish. Can't control the weather. All you can do is show up, be present, and see what happens."

Bear nodded, understanding. "Kind of the opposite of football, where everything is timed, measured, controlled."

"Exactly. That's why balance matters—different activities engage different parts of us. If all you do is one thing, no matter how well you do it, parts of you go dormant."

As they drove home, Bear felt more relaxed than he had in months. The morning on the lake had refreshed something in him that he hadn't realized needed refreshing—a capacity for stillness, for presence, for simply being rather than constantly doing or becoming.

That afternoon, at Akeem's cookout, Bear focused on enjoying his teammates as people—laughing at jokes, joining the volleyball game in the pool, and even jumping in to help Akeem's father at the grill.

"You seem different," Tyler observed as they sat on the deck, watching some of the younger players engage in an increasingly competitive diving contest. "More relaxed today than usual."

"I really want to find better balance," Bear explained. "Excellence in football and school, but not at the cost of everything else."

Tyler nodded. "I get that. Sometimes I wonder if I've missed out on the normal high school experience, being so focused on football."

"It's not too late," Bear pointed out. "You've still got most of your senior year ahead of you."

"True," Tyler agreed. "Though with college recruiting and everything . . ."

"It'll always be something," Bear said, echoing his father's wisdom. "There's always a reason to be all in on one thing at the expense of everything else. But that doesn't mean it's always the right choice."

When Bear met with Tony for their next session, he shared what he'd been learning about balance and its importance.

"I went fishing with my dad," Bear told him. "And I realized how much I'd been missing by being so singularly focused. Not just the activity itself, but the change of pace and the different perspective it brings."

Tony nodded. "That's wisdom, Bear. Excellence isn't about being one-dimensional. It's about being your best self in all dimensions of life."

"But how do you maintain that level of balance consistently?" Bear asked. "There are only so many hours in a day."

"It's not about perfect balance all the time," Tony clarified. "It's about rhythm—seasons of intensity followed by seasons of recovery, seasons of focus followed by seasons of broader engagement. The key is intentionality—choosing your emphasis rather than letting circumstances choose for you."

He picked up a football. "Think of it like a quarterback's progression. You have primary targets, secondary options, check-downs. You don't force the ball to your first read if it's covered. You go through your progression, finding the best option for that specific situation."

Bear nodded, understanding the analogy. "So right now, football and academics might be my primary reads, but I still need to scan the field, stay aware of other options, and other aspects of life."

"Exactly," Tony confirmed. "And sometimes, the best play is to check down to a relationship, a hobby, a moment of rest. Not because they're less important, but because they're what's open in that moment."

Over the next few weeks, Bear worked on implementing this more balanced approach. He still maintained his commitment to excellence in football and academics, but he also made space for other priorities:

- Sunday afternoons became protected family time, with no studying or film review allowed.
- Once a week, he and Heather spent their study session talking about non-academic interests.

- He joined a group text with friends who weren't on the football team, keeping those connections alive.
- He started leaving his phone in another room during dinner, giving his parents his full attention.

In his journal, Bear tracked these adjustments:

Today's Game: Building a life of balanced excellence

My Competition: The tendency to make football and academics my entire identity

Why It Matters: Because true excellence includes how we engage with all aspects of life

Touching the line doesn't always look like adding more—sometimes it looks like setting boundaries, creating space, being fully present in non-achievement contexts. The one-degree difference can be about intensity of focus, but it can also be about quality of presence.

As October progressed, Bear found that this more balanced approach wasn't diminishing his performance—it was enhancing it. He came to practices and study sessions more refreshed, more focused, more creative. The mental and emotional space created by other activities gave his primary pursuits room to breathe and develop.

"You're practicing better than you have all season, Bear," Coach Turner observed after a particularly sharp practice. "Just as focused, but you seem more relaxed. What's changed?"

Bear considered the question. "I've been working on balance, Coach. Making sure football stays my top priority but doesn't crowd out everything else in my life."

Coach nodded. "The best athletes I've coached have always had that balance— something else they care about besides their sport. Keeps them grounded, gives them perspective."

When he got home that night, Bear turned to his journal one more time:

I'm beginning to understand that the greatest excellence isn't found in single-minded pursuit of one goal at the expense of everything else. It's found in the balanced development of all my capacities—athletic, intellectual, relational, and spiritual.

Maybe touching the line is as much about boundaries as it is about effort—knowing when to push and when to rest, when to focus and when to expand, when to strive and when to simply be.

I'm starting to think that the most challenging line to touch is the extra inch that separates a life of achievement from a life of meaning.

CHAPTER 12
THE SLUMP

"Wilson! A word, please."

Coach Turner's voice carried across the practice field as the team finished their warmup stretches. It was early November, with playoff preparations in full swing. Tyler had injured his shoulder in the first quarter of the previous game, and despite feeling better, the trainers were limiting him this week to light throwing—which meant Bear would be the starting quarterback for at least this week.

"Yes, Coach?" Bear asked, jogging over.

Coach Turner gestured to a freshman standing beside him—a slender boy with an athletic build who Bear immediately recognized as the young quarterback who had been watching his practice sessions with Tony over the summer. The one who had studied Bear's movements with unusual intensity from beyond the fence line.

"This is Max Jenkins. Freshman team quarterback. He's going to be practicing with varsity for the rest of the season."

Bear nodded a greeting and said, "Hey, Max."

"Max has got a ton of natural talent," Coach continued, "but he needs to learn our system, our expectations. I want you to take him under your wing—show him the ropes, help him understand how we do things at the varsity level."

Bear was caught off guard. With playoffs approaching and his own responsibilities as starting quarterback, mentoring a freshman hadn't been on his radar. But he remembered how Tony had invested in him, how that guidance had transformed not just his performance but his entire approach to excellence.

"Happy to," Bear replied. "When do you want me to start?"

"Today," Coach said. "Have him shadow you during position drills. Explain what we're doing and why."

As Coach walked away, Bear turned to Max, who seemed both excited and intimidated by his sudden promotion to varsity practice.

"So, quarterback, huh?" Bear said, trying to put the freshman at ease.

Max nodded. "Yeah. Been playing since I was seven."

"You've had a good season with the freshman team," Bear observed. "I caught parts of a few of y'all's scores."

"Ten touchdowns, two interceptions," Max replied with a confidence that bordered on cockiness. "Coach says I might get to dress for the playoff game Friday."

Bear nodded, getting a clearer picture of what he was dealing with—natural talent coupled with the unearned confidence of someone who'd been the best player on every team he'd ever played for. He'd seen it before, and in some ways, it reminded him of Tyler earlier in the season.

"Well, stick with me today," Bear said. "Varsity's a different game. Faster, more complex. But you'll catch on."

During quarterback drills, Bear took time to explain each exercise—the footwork, the reads, the timing. Max was clearly athletic, with a strong arm and quick feet, but Bear noticed something concerning: the freshman often rushed through drills, skipping steps or cutting corners when he thought no one was watching.

After one particular footwork drill where Max had glossed over the final progression, Bear pulled him aside.

"You need to complete all five steps," Bear said quietly. "Not just the first three."

Max looked surprised, then defensive. "Does it really matter? I still made the throw."

"It matters," Bear said firmly. "Especially when you think it doesn't."

Max rolled his eyes. "Look, I appreciate you trying to help, but I've been making these throws since I was nine. My dad says too much technique talk gets in a quarterback's head."

Bear felt a sense of déjà vu, remembering his own resistance to "touching the line" when Tony had first called him out.

"Maybe that works at the freshman level," he said. "But at varsity, the margins get thinner. The difference between completion and interception isn't just arm talent—it's precision. And precision comes from discipline."

"Whatever," Max muttered, clearly unconvinced but unwilling to argue further with an upperclassman.

Throughout the practice, Bear continued to observe Max. The freshman had undeniable talent—a natural throwing motion, good instincts, and the kind of confidence that could either be his greatest asset or his ultimate downfall, depending on how it was channeled.

But he also had concerning habits: taking shortcuts, rushing through mechanical drills to get to the "fun" parts of practice, showing little interest in the mental aspects of the position.

After practice, as the team headed to the locker room, Bear approached Coach Turner. "What do you think of Jenkins?" Coach asked before Bear could speak.

"Talented," Bear replied honestly. "Great arm, good athlete. But—"

"But he takes shortcuts," Coach interjected. "Thinks he can get by on natural ability alone."

Bear nodded, relieved that Coach had seen it too. "Exactly."

"Remind you of anyone?" Coach asked with a knowing look.

Bear thought immediately of Tyler earlier in the season, but then realized Coach might also be referring to him—to his own journey from technique-focused backup to complete quarterback.

"That's why I want you working with him," Coach continued. "You've learned what he needs to learn. And sometimes peers can reach these kids in ways coaches can't."

Bear nodded, accepting the challenge. "Yes sir, I'll do my best."

"I know you will," Coach said. "That's why I asked you and not Greene. Tyler's a great quarterback, but you understand the journey from where Max is to where he needs to be."

The next day, Bear arrived at practice early, hoping to catch Max before the team warm-ups. Sure enough, the freshman was on the field, throwing to one of the JV receivers. But as Bear watched, he noticed something concerning: Max's footwork was sloppy, his mechanics inconsistent. He was focused solely on the result—completing the pass—with little attention to the process.

"Got a minute?" Bear called, walking onto the field.

Max turned, surprised. "Uh, sure."

"Your arm talent is obvious," Bear began, deciding on directness. "But your footwork needs work."

Max's expression shifted from surprise to a full defensive posture. "I complete my passes."

"Against freshman defenses, sure," Bear acknowledged. "But at varsity level, those windows get a lot smaller. The margin for error shrinks. Suddenly, those inconsistencies start showing up as incompletions or interceptions."

He demonstrated the proper footwork for a 5-step drop, then asked Max to mirror him. The freshman complied, but with a halfhearted effort that suggested he was just going through the motions to appease an upperclassman.

"You don't really believe this matters, do you?" Bear asked, recognizing the attitude.

"Look," Max said with visible frustration, "I've always been able to make the throws. My dad says technique is overrated—that the great ones have natural ability you can't teach. And

I'm not trying to be rude, but I've seen you play. You're good because you work at it. I'm good because I just am."

The comment stung, but Bear recognized the defense mechanism—the ego protection that came from a young athlete who'd never truly been challenged. He'd been there himself, in different ways.

"Your dad's partly right," Bear said calmly. "Natural ability matters. But it's not enough—not at the higher levels."

"Seems to be working for me so far," Max replied with the unshakable confidence of someone who'd never experienced real failure.

Instead of arguing, Bear changed tactics. "How about this? After practice today, let's have a little competition. Accuracy challenge. If I win, you commit to working on the fundamentals I show you, no shortcuts. If you win, I'll back off."

Max's competitive instinct was immediately piqued. "What kind of challenge?"

"Ten throws each, hitting targets at different spots on the field. Highest score wins."

"You're on," Max said, clearly confident in his ability to outthrow the upperclassman.

After team practice, Bear set up the challenge. He placed hula hoops at various distances and angles on the field, each worth different points based on difficulty. Coach Turner, curious about the setup, stopped to watch along with a few lingering players.

Max went first, showcasing his impressive arm talent. His throws had zip and good accuracy, but his mechanics were inconsistent. Still, he managed to hit seven of the ten targets, finishing with 28 points.

"Not bad," Bear acknowledged. "My turn."

With deliberate focus, Bear worked through his ten throws. His mechanics were consistent, his footwork precise. He hit nine of the ten targets, finishing with 37 points.

"That's game," Coach Turner called with a slight smile.

Max looked both impressed and slightly deflated. "How did you hit that back corner target? It's almost impossible."

"Consistent mechanics," Bear replied. "When your footwork and release point are the same every time, you develop muscle memory. Then when you need precision, it's there."

He tossed a ball to Max. "So, do we have a deal? You work on the fundamentals, no shortcuts?"

Max hesitated, his ego clearly battling with the evidence before him. Finally, he nodded. "Deal. But I want a rematch in a month."

"You're on," Bear said. "But I should warn you: If you actually work on your mechanics, you might beat me next time."

Over the next few weeks, Bear spent time before and after practice working with Max. The freshman remained resistant, often arguing about the necessity of certain drills or question ing Bear's instruction.

But gradually, Bear began to see changes. Max's footwork became more disciplined, his mechanics more consistent, his attention to detail more focused.

As Bear's mentorship of Max became more visible, something unexpected happened. Other players began approaching Bear with questions—not just about football techniques, but about his approach to preparation, to balancing academics and athletics, to handling the pressures of being a starter.

"How do you stay so calm in the huddle?" asked Rodriguez, a sophomore receiver who had been elevated to the varsity squad. "Even when we're down, you never seem rattled."

"It's about perspective," Bear explained, sharing some of Tony's wisdom about the bigger game. "Football matters, but it's not the only thing that matters. And when you prepare thoroughly, you trust that preparation under pressure."

WHEN YOU PREPARE THOROUGHLY, YOU TRUST THAT PREPARATION UNDER PRESSURE.

After one particularly demanding practice, Marcus, a junior lineman who had struggled with consistency all season, approached Bear in the weight room.

"Wilson, you got a minute? I've been watching how you approach practice. There's something different about it. Like, even the boring drills, you do them like they're game reps."

Bear smiled, recognizing another opportunity to pass along what he'd learned. "That's exactly it. Excellence isn't just about the highlight reel stuff. It's about all the small choices that lead up to those moments. The one-degree difference between water and ice."

"Water and ice?" Marcus asked, confused.

Bear explained Tony's analogy, about how just one degree separated liquid from solid, how small, consistent choices compounded over time to create transformation.

"So you're saying if I approach every drill, every rep, every practice with that same level of focus—"

"It changes everything," Bear confirmed. "Not overnight. But over time, absolutely."

One afternoon, as Bear worked with Max on reading progressions, he decided to share some of Tony's broader wisdom.

"You know, football's not the only place where these principles matter," he told Max as they reviewed coverage recognition. "The habits you build now—attention to detail, completing every rep with purpose, no shortcuts—they show up in everything else too."

Max looked skeptical. "Like what?"

"School. Relationships. Whatever career you choose. The approach is the same."

"My dad says football is going to be my career," Max said with the certainty only a fourteen-year-old could muster. "So that's all that really matters."

Bear recognized the narrow thinking, remembering his own single-minded focus earlier in the season. "And what if it isn't? What if you get injured? Or what if you make it to college but not beyond?"

Max shrugged, clearly uncomfortable with the questions. "I don't think about that."

"Maybe you should," Bear suggested gently. "Not because it will happen, but because being prepared for multiple paths is smarter than betting everything on just one."

They were interrupted by Tyler, who had been watching from the sideline. His arm was completely healed and ready for practice.

“Mind if I join you guys?” Tyler asked.

“Not at all,” Bear replied, genuinely pleased to see Tyler more involved. “We’re working on progression reads.”

For the next thirty minutes, the three quarterbacks worked together: Bear and Tyler demonstrating and explaining, Max observing and practicing. It was a natural, unforced mentoring session, with the older players sharing what they knew and the younger one soaking it up.

As they finished, Max surprised them both by asking, “How do you two do it?”

“Do what?” Tyler asked.

“Work together like this,” Max clarified. “You’re competing for the same position. Shouldn’t you be trying to make each other look bad, not helping each other?”

Bear and Tyler exchanged a glance, a moment of unspoken understanding passing between them.

“That’s what we thought at first too,” Tyler admitted. “But we figured out that we make each other better by competing with each other, not against each other.”

“Iron sharpens iron,” Bear added. “When he pushes me, I improve. When I push him, he improves. The team gets two better quarterbacks instead of one.”

Max looked thoughtful, as if encountering a new concept. “My dad always says second place is just the first loser.”

“No offense,” Tyler said carefully, “but your dad’s perspective might be limiting you. There’s more to learn from this game than just who starts and who sits.”

After Max left, Tyler turned to Bear. "Kid's got a ton of talent."

"And an ego to match," Bear added.

Tyler laughed. "Remind you of anyone?"

"Both of us, at different times," Bear acknowledged. "He's got your natural ability and my initial resistance to the deeper lessons."

"Good thing he has us to set him straight," Tyler said. "Though I don't envy you the task."

As the Panthers prepared for their first playoff game, Bear noticed something unexpected: Max was arriving early for practice that week, working on the fundamentals they'd discussed before the team sessions even began. The freshman still had his moments of cockiness, still occasionally tried to get by on talent alone, but there was a noticeable shift in his approach.

By now, Bear's leadership influence had spread beyond Max. Several players had taken to staying after practice for extra work, seeking Bear out for advice not just on techniques but on mindset. Even Coach Turner had noticed the change in team culture.

"Wilson," he said one day after a particularly sharp practice, "I'm seeing a different energy with this team lately. More focus. More attention to detail. Your influence is spreading."

Bear felt a sense of pride at the observation, but also an awareness of responsibility. He was no longer just working on his own improvement; he was helping shape the culture of the entire team.

After one particularly productive session where Max had executed a complex progression read correctly, Bear offered genuine praise: "You're getting it. That's exactly right."

Max seemed pleased but tried to downplay it. "It's not that hard once you explain it."

"True," Bear agreed. "But you have to be willing to listen in the first place. Not everyone is."

Max hesitated, then asked, "Were you always good at this stuff? The details, the preparation?"

Bear laughed. "Not even close. I've been learning just like you are now. The difference is, I had someone teaching me too."

"Coach Turner?"

"He's taught me a lot," Bear acknowledged. "But I was thinking of Tony Brewer. Former quarterback here, state champion back in the day. He's been mentoring me all season."

"What does he tell you?" Max asked, curiosity breaking through his usual veneer of confidence.

Bear thought about how to distill months of guidance into a concise message. "He taught me that excellence isn't just about talent or even hard work. It's about the small choices—touching the line when you're tired, completing every rep with purpose, understanding that how you do one thing is how you do everything."

He picked up a football, turning it in his hands. "Tony calls it the extra-inch difference. You know how water freezes at thirty-two degrees? At thirty-three, it's still liquid. Just one degree changes everything.

"That's what these small choices are—the extra inch that transforms good to great, potential to achievement."

THE HABITS YOU BUILD NOW WILL EITHER LIFT YOUR CEILING OR LIMIT IT.

Max was quiet for a moment, absorbing this. "And that's why you're so focused on me not cutting corners in drills."

"Exactly," Bear confirmed. "Because the habits you build now will either lift your ceiling or limit it. And not just in football."

The next day, Bear arrived at practice to find Max already on the field—not just throwing, but deliberately working through the footwork drills Bear had taught him, with focused attention to detail that hadn't been there before.

"Morning," Bear called. "You're here early."

"Figured I should touch the line," Max replied with a small smile that suggested he was both embracing the concept and gently mocking it.

Bear laughed. "Well, look at you, using the lingo and everything."

As they worked together, Bear was struck by how teaching these principles to Max was deepening his own understanding of them. Explaining the "why" behind each drill, each technique, and each approach was forcing him to clarify his own thinking, to internalize the lessons more fully.

"You know what's weird?" Bear said as they took a water break. "Teaching you is actually making me better too."

"How's that?" Max asked.

"It forces me to really understand what I'm doing and why. When it's just me, I can sometimes go on autopilot. But when I have to explain it to someone else, I have to be clear about the purpose, the process, the principles."

Max nodded thoughtfully. "My dad always says you don't really know something until you can teach it."

"Your dad's right about that," Bear acknowledged. "Maybe he's not wrong about everything."

Max smiled slightly. "He loves football. Wants me to go further than he did. He played in college but got injured junior year."

"That explains a lot," Bear said, understanding better now why Max's father pushed him so hard in some ways while overlooking the fundamental details that might actually help him achieve those ambitions.

"Yeah," Max agreed. "Sometimes I think he's trying to live his dream through me."

The vulnerability in the admission surprised Bear, as it broke through the freshman's carefully maintained facade of cocky self-assurance.

"That's a lot of pressure to put on a fourteen-year-old," Bear observed.

Max shrugged, trying to reclaim his nonchalance. "I can handle it."

"I'm sure you can," Bear agreed. "But you don't have to handle it alone. That's what teammates are for. What mentors are for."

As they returned to drills, Bear noticed a subtle shift in Max's demeanor—a little less bravado, a little more genuine engagement with the process. The walls were coming down, bit by bit.

Later that week, as the Panthers prepared for their second playoff game, Coach Turner called Bear aside after practice.

"I've been watching you work with Jenkins," he said. "You're doing good work there." "Thanks, Coach. He's coming along."

"It's more than that," Coach countered. "You're teaching him things he needs to hear from someone other than a coach. And from what I can see, you're learning just as much from the process."

Bear nodded, surprised by Coach's perceptiveness. "I am. Having to explain why things matter forces me to clarify my own understanding."

"That's how it works," Coach said with a knowing smile. "Teaching is the highest form of learning. That's why I asked you to mentor him—not just for his benefit, but for yours."

As Coach walked away, Akeem approached, slapping Bear on the shoulder. "Man, Wilson, what's gotten into you? First you're like some Zen-master quarterback, now you're Professor Wilson teaching the rookies."

Bear laughed. "Just passing along what I've learned."

"Well, it's working," Akeem said more seriously. "The team's different. You're different. Heck, even I'm different. All this 'touch the line' and 'extra inch' stuff—it's getting into my head too."

Bear felt a deep satisfaction at his friend's words. The principles weren't just changing him; they were rippling outward, affecting others, creating a culture of excellence that went beyond any individual.

In his journal that night, Bear reflected on this new dimension of his journey:

Today's Game: Mentoring a young quarterback while continuing to grow myself

My Competition: The temptation to keep knowledge to myself rather than sharing it

Why It Matters: Because true excellence isn't just about personal achievement but about elevating others

I'm learning that touching the line has a communal aspect I hadn't considered before. It's not just about my discipline or my growth—it's about creating an environment where everyone touches the line, where excellence becomes the standard rather than the exception.

And there's something powerful about the cycle of learning and teaching—how receiving wisdom creates a responsibility to pass it on, how explaining principles to others deepens your own understanding of them.

Maybe this is the ultimate expression of the one-degree difference—not just personal transformation, but transformation that ripples outward, changing the temperature around you until others begin to freeze too, solid in their commitment to excellence.

As the Panthers continued their playoff run, Bear noticed Max becoming more integrated with the varsity team. The freshman still had his moments of cockiness, still occasionally tried to rely solely on his natural talent, but there was a growing receptiveness to coaching, a developing attention to detail that hadn't been there before.

More importantly, Max was beginning to understand that his development as a quarterback wasn't separate from his development as a person—that the principles of excellence applied across all domains of life.

That night, as Bear reviewed game film for the upcoming quarterfinal match, his phone buzzed with a text from Tony:

Meet me at the Historical Society tomorrow at 4 p.m. There's something I want to show you.

Bear stared at the message, puzzled. In all their meetings, they'd never gone to the Historical Society, a place Bear had visited only on elementary school field trips. What could Tony possibly want to show him there? And why now, with the biggest game of the season just days away?

Despite his confusion, Bear texted back a simple *Okay.* Tony had never steered him wrong before. Whatever this was about, Bear trusted it was important.

As he returned to his film study, Bear couldn't help but wonder if he was about to discover another layer to the principles that had transformed his life over the past several months.

CHAPTER 13
THE MENTOR'S STORY

The Jackson Creek Historical Society was a small but well-maintained building near the town square. Most residents rarely visited except for the annual Founders' Day celebration or when elementary school classes took field trips to learn about local history.

Bear pulled into the nearly empty parking lot, wondering why Tony had asked to meet him here instead of their usual spots. It was a Wednesday afternoon in mid-November, with the Panthers preparing for their quarterfinal playoff game that Friday.

But Tony's text last night hadn't mentioned football.

Inside, the building was quiet, the only sound coming from a desk fan oscillating gently in the corner where an elderly volunteer dozed behind a reception desk. She startled awake as the door closed behind Bear.

"Oh! Hello, young man. Can I help you?"

"I'm meeting someone . . . Tony Brewer?"

"Ah, yes. He's in the sports gallery, second door on the right."

Bear followed her directions down a short hallway decorated with black-and-white photographs of Jackson Creek's early days—lumber mills, railroad construction, the first town council. The sports gallery, when he entered it, was a modest room featuring display cases of trophies, jerseys, and memorabilia from the town's athletic history.

Tony stood before a glass case containing a faded jersey—number 12—and various newspaper clippings yellowed with age. He turned as Bear approached.

"Thanks for coming," Tony said. "Especially on a busy week."

"No problem," Bear replied. "Though I'm curious why we're meeting here."

Tony gestured to the display. "Because I think it's time you heard my story. The full version, not just the one in the trophy case."

Bear moved closer, studying the items in the case. The centerpiece was Tony's jersey from the state championship team twenty years earlier. Surrounding it were newspaper headlines: "Brewer Leads Panthers to State Title," "Miracle in the Final Seconds," and "Division I Schools Courting Local Star."

"Everyone in town knows this part of the story," Tony said, pointing to the display. "How we went 15-0, how I threw the winning touchdown in the state final with no time left on the clock."

Bear nodded. It was a legend in Jackson Creek, repeated almost as folklore.

"What they don't know," Tony continued, moving to another display case, "is what happened after."

This case contained fewer items—a college program with Tony's picture circled, a few more modest news clippings, a Texas Tech jersey emblazoned with the number 12.

"I got a scholarship to play at Texas Tech," Tony explained. "Everyone expected me to be a star there too. But it didn't work out that way."

He pointed to one of the news clippings: "Brewer Shows Promise in Spring Game."

"That was the high point of my college career," Tony said with a wry smile. "A spring scrimmage my freshman year. By sophomore year, I was third string. By junior year, I was considering transferring. By senior year, I was just going through the motions, waiting for it to be over."

Bear was surprised. This wasn't the story he'd heard growing up. In Jackson Creek lore, Tony Brewer had been a hometown hero who'd gone on to college glory. The reality seemed much different.

"What happened?" Bear asked. "Did you get injured?"

Tony nodded grimly. "Torn labrum in the final game of our championship season. Required surgery and months of rehab."

He motioned for Bear to follow him to a small conference room adjacent to the gallery. Inside, a table displayed more artifacts—medical reports, rehabilitation schedules, playbooks, training schedules, handwritten notes.

"In high school, I was a lot like you," Tony explained as they sat down. "Not the most naturally gifted quarterback on the team, but I outworked everyone. I was gritty, smart, and studied harder than anyone else. I found ways to compete against players who had better arms, faster feet, stronger bodies."

"But you're the one who taught me about touching the line," Bear said, confused.

"I learned it the hard way," Tony replied. "Because back then, I didn't have the frameworks. I didn't understand what game I was really playing."

He spread out some of the medical reports and rehabilitation schedules. "I went to Texas Tech thinking I could outwork everyone there too. But while I was rehabbing that first semester, spending hours alone in the weight room, watching more talented players learn the playbook and earn reps I couldn't take . . . something broke inside me."

Bear was quiet, trying to reconcile this image with the wise, grounded mentor he'd come to know.

"My entire identity was wrapped up in being the quarterback," Tony continued. "The guy who found a way to win despite not having the biggest arm or the fastest legs. But suddenly, I was facing a reality I'd never confronted—what if my best wasn't good enough at this level?"

He pointed to a medical clearance form. "By the time I was physically ready to compete, mentally I was already defeated. I'd spent months watching another quarterback—kid had a cannon for an arm, would go on to play over a decade in the NFL—and I convinced myself I could never measure up."

"You got depressed?" Bear asked, slowly grasping the deeper struggle.

"Completely," Tony confirmed. "Because I was competing against everyone else instead of competing against my own potential. I was so focused on what I couldn't control—other players' talent—that I stopped controlling what I could. I stopped going the extra inch when no one was watching because I'd convinced myself it wouldn't matter anyway."

He spread out some of the items on the table—course syllabi and academic reports alongside football playbooks. "I wasn't just unprepared mentally. I was unprepared for the academic rigors, for living away from home, for managing my time and priorities while dealing with depression and fear."

"So what happened?" Bear asked, fascinated by this untold chapter of Tony's story.

"I floundered," Tony admitted. "My confidence eroded. I blamed my injury, timing, coaches—anyone but myself—for my failures. I developed a chip on my shoulder, an entitlement mentality. The Tony Brewer who left Jackson Creek was not the same person who limped back four years later."

Bear was quiet, trying to reconcile this image with the wise, grounded mentor he'd come to know. "Something must have changed," he observed.

"Something did," Tony confirmed. "Or rather, someone helped me change."

He picked up a piece of paper—what looked like a handwritten letter. "My senior year, I was just going through the motions. I knew I wasn't going pro after college or even play that final season. I had no real career plans. I was taking easy classes to maintain eligibility, even though I didn't play."

He handed the letter to Bear. "Then, I got this from Coach Turner."

Bear looked up in surprise. "Our Coach Turner?"

Tony nodded. "He was just starting his coaching career back then. Had been a graduate assistant at Texas Tech when I first arrived. He'd moved on to coach high school, but we stayed in touch."

Bear carefully unfolded the letter, brittle with age:

Tony,

I've been hearing about your situation from mutual contacts at Tech. I'm sorry things haven't worked out as you hoped on the football front. But I'm more concerned about what I'm hearing about your attitude, your academic effort, and your general direction—you're better than this, Tony.

The young man I recruited from Jackson Creek wasn't just a good quarterback—he was a leader, a person of character, someone who lifted others around him. I don't know what's happened since then, but I do know this: How you respond to disappointment will define your character far more than how you handle success.

Football was never going to last forever, even if you'd become a star at Tech or gone pro. It's a vehicle, not a destination—a means of developing discipline, teamwork, perseverance, and other qualities that serve you long after the game is over. If you've lost sight of that, you've missed the real value of the sport.

It's not too late to finish strong, to extract meaning and growth from this experience, to prepare yourself for whatever comes next. But that choice is yours alone.

Remember what we talked about during recruitment—it's not about being the best on the team, it's about being the best for the team. That principle applies beyond football, to whatever community or organization you're part of next.

I believe in you, Tony. Not because of your position or your athleticism, but because of the character I saw in that eighteen-year-old from Jackson Creek. That young man is still in there. I hope he finds his way forward.

—Coach Turner

Bear finished reading, moved by the directness and compassion in Coach Turner's words. It gave him a new perspective on the gruff but fair-minded coach he'd known these past few years.

"That letter hit me hard," Tony admitted. "Partly because it came from someone I respected, but mostly because it was true. I'd lost my way. I'd forgotten why I played in the first place. I'd allowed disappointment and fear to corrupt my character rather than strengthen it."

"What did you do?" Bear asked.

"I changed course completely," Tony replied. "For my final semester, I committed to being the best teammate possible, even though I knew I wouldn't play. I rededicated myself academically, bringing my grades up significantly. I started mentoring younger players, sharing what I'd learned—both what to do and what not to do."

He smiled slightly. "And a funny thing happened. Once I stopped obsessing over playing time and started focusing on personal growth, I actually enjoyed football again. I became a leader in a different way—through example, through service to the team."

Bear nodded, understanding the parallel to his own journey with Tyler. "But you never got to be the starter again?"

"No," Tony acknowledged. "And that was a hard pill to swallow at first. But I learned something invaluable: Success isn't just about outcomes or positions. It's about who you become in the process."

He gathered the items on the table, returning them carefully to their folders. "After college, I came back here with a chip on my shoulder. Felt like a failure returning to my small town after dreams of glory had faded."

"What changed?" Bear asked.

"Time. Perspective. And finding purpose beyond football," Tony answered. "I got an engineering degree along with my football experience. Found I had an aptitude for problem-solving, systems thinking. Landed a job with an energy company in Houston, did well there."

"So why did you come back to Jackson Creek?" Bear asked, curious about the part of the story he didn't know.

"My mother got sick," Tony explained. "Alzheimer's. I moved back to help care for her during her final years. Thought it would be temporary, but after she passed, I found I wanted to stay. This town had given me so much—it felt right to give something back."

He stood, gesturing for Bear to follow him back into the sports gallery. "When I first moved back, I avoided anything to do with football. Too many complicated feelings. But then Coach Turner approached me about mentoring some of his players. Said my experience—both the success and the failure—gave me a perspective these kids needed."

They stopped before the championship jersey again. "I was reluctant at first. Wasn't sure I had anything to offer. But Coach insisted. Said sometimes the best teachers are those who've experienced both the heights and the depths."

"Is that when you developed the frameworks?" Bear asked. "COMPETE and TODAY?"

Tony nodded. "They evolved over time, from working with different players, from reading and studying leadership principles, from my own reflection on what I'd learned through success and failure."

He turned to face Bear directly. "That first day on the field, when I saw you running sprints alone after practice, I recognized something in you—a drive, a determination—but also a vulnerability to the same pitfalls that caught me. And when I saw you cut that corner, not touching the line when you thought no one was watching, I knew I needed to intervene."

"I'm glad you did," Bear said sincerely.

Tony smiled. "Me too. But here's what I want you to understand, Bear. The frameworks, the principles, the concepts like going the extra inch—they're not just about football success. They're about building character that lasts long after the stadium lights go dark."

He gestured to a final display case, one Bear hadn't noticed before. It contained not sports memorabilia but community service awards, engineering patents, and photographs of Tony with local youth groups.

"This is my real legacy," Tony said quietly. "Not the championship, not the statistics, but the lives I've been able to impact since football ended. And it all started with that letter from Coach Turner, reminding me that how I responded to disappointment would define my character far more than how I handled success."

Bear absorbed this, seeing Tony in a new light. Not just as a former football star, not even just as a mentor, but as someone who had faced failure, learned from it, and found meaning beyond the scoreboard.

"That's why these frameworks matter so much," Tony continued. "If I'd understood then what I'm teaching you now—that the real competition is against yourself, that excellence is built in the margins, that your worth isn't determined by your position on a depth chart—everything could have been different."

"So the quarterfinal game this Friday," Bear said slowly. "Whether I start or Tyler does—"

"It matters, but not in the way you might think," Tony interjected. "It's an opportunity either way—to lead, to grow, to touch the line when it's hardest. And the real victory won't be measured on the scoreboard, but in who you're becoming through the process."

As they left the Historical Society, walking into the crisp November afternoon, Bear felt a clarity he hadn't expected. The uncertainty about Friday's game suddenly seemed less weighty, less defining. Whatever role he played, the opportunity to compete—to bring his best self to the moment—would be there.

"One more thing," Tony said as they reached their cars. "Coach Turner hasn't told me his plan for Friday. But whatever it is, I want you to know this: I'm proud of the young man you're becoming, Bear. Not because of touchdowns or wins, but because of your growth in character, in perspective, in understanding what really matters."

The words touched Bear deeply, reminding him of his mother's similar affirmation. To be valued not for what he did but for who he was becoming—that was a different kind of recognition, one that resonated at a deeper level than any athletic accolade.

"Thanks, Tony," he said simply. "For everything."

That evening, as Bear studied film in preparation for Friday's game, his phone buzzed with a text from Coach Turner: *My office, 7:30 a.m. tomorrow.*

Bear felt the familiar flutter of anticipation, but it was different now, tempered by perspective, by understanding that whatever decision came, it would be another opportunity to touch the line, to demonstrate the character he was developing.

In his journal that night, he wrote:

Today's Game: Understanding the bigger picture beyond football

My Competition: The belief that my value is tied to my performance or position

Why It Matters: Because who I become through this process is more important than any win or loss

Tony's story changed how I see all of this. Touching the line isn't just about being disciplined to achieve success—it's about being disciplined because that discipline shapes who I am becoming. And that's a game I can win regardless of what happens on the scoreboard.

Whether I play on Friday or not, I'll have opportunities to lead, to elevate others, to bring my best self to whatever role I have. And in a strange way, knowing Tony's full story—both the triumph and the struggle—makes me more prepared for either outcome.

The one-degree difference isn't just between winning and losing; it's between allowing circumstances to define you and choosing to define yourself through how you respond to those circumstances.

The next morning, Bear arrived at Coach Turner's office early, determined to accept whatever decision had been made with maturity and perspective.

Coach was already there, reviewing game plans at his desk. He looked up as Bear entered. "Close the door and have a seat, Wilson."

Bear did as instructed, his heart rate picking up despite his philosophical reflections of the previous evening.

"I've been thinking a lot about Friday's game," Coach began. "Greene's back to one hundred percent. His shoulder has healed well. By traditional coaching standards, that would mean he automatically returns to his starting role."

He leaned forward. "But I've also been watching you develop all season—not just as a quarterback, but as a leader, a young man of character. The way you've handled the competition with Tyler, the way you bounced back from that slump, the way you've mentored Max Jenkins."

Bear waited, not wanting to make assumptions about where this was heading.

"So here's what we're going to do," Coach continued. "Greene will start on Friday. He's earned that as a senior and because of the quality of his time here, and he's healthy enough to play."

Bear felt a twinge of disappointment but nodded his acceptance.

"But," Coach added, "you'll have a much larger role than the package plays we were using earlier in the season. I'm planning to rotate you in for full series, not just specific situations. I want to keep the defense guessing, and I want to use the unique strengths both of you bring."

He studied Bear's reaction. "How do you feel about that?"

Bear considered the question honestly. "If you'd asked me at the beginning of the season, I would have been disappointed with anything less than the full starting role. But now, I see it differently. It's not about the position; it's about making the most of whatever opportunities I have to contribute."

Coach nodded, seeming pleased with the response. "That's growth, Wilson. That's maturity. And it's why, regardless of how the depth chart reads, I consider you every bit as much a leader of this team as Greene."

He stood, signaling the end of the meeting. "One more thing. I'm glad Tony shared his story with you yesterday."

Bear looked up in surprise. "You knew about that?"

"I suggested it," Coach admitted. "Thought you were ready to hear the full version, not just the highlight reel. We all need to understand that success and failure are both teachers—if we're willing to learn from them."

As Bear left the office and headed to his first-period class, he felt a sense of peace that transcended the coaching decision. He was still competitive, still wanted to play, still believed in his abilities. But now those desires were framed within a larger perspective—one that valued growth over status, character over accolades, process over position.

And in that perspective, he found freedom—to play without the crushing pressure of defining his worth by his role, to lead without the insecurity of constantly comparing himself to others, to touch the line not for recognition but because that's who he was becoming.

Friday's game would be important, certainly. But the more significant contest had already been won—the internal battle to align his ambitions with his character, to find meaning beyond the scoreboard, to understand that touching the line was ultimately about who he was, not just what he did.

THE REAL COMPETITION WAS THE DAILY CHOICE TO BECOME HIS BEST SELF.

And in that understanding, Bear Wilson was becoming something more valuable than a starting quarterback: he was becoming a young man of substance, of perspective, of character that would serve him long after his final snap of football.

Tony had been right all along. The real competition wasn't against Tyler Greene or any external opponent. It was the daily choice to become the best version of himself, one small decision at a time.

CHAPTER 14
PLAYOFF CRUCIBLE

The stadium lights cast long shadows across the field as Bear completed his pregame warmup routine. This wasn't Jackson Creek's home field but a neutral site—a college stadium about two hours away—chosen for the quarterfinal playoff game against Westlake, a perennial powerhouse with three state titles in the past decade.

The stands were filling rapidly, a sea of red and gray on the Westlake side contrasting with the blue and gold of Jackson Creek supporters. Bear spotted his parents in the visitors' section, his father's familiar letter jacket visible even from the field. A few rows away sat Tony, deep in conversation with several other Jackson Creek alumni who had made the journey.

In the locker room earlier, Coach Turner's pregame speech had been characteristically straightforward: "You've earned the right to be here. Not because you're the most talented team in the bracket, but because you've outworked, out-prepared, and out-executed your opponents. Tonight will test everything we've built the past thirteen weeks—our discipline, our unity, our resilience. Trust your training. Trust each other. Win one play at a time."

Now, as the team gathered for final instructions before kickoff, Coach addressed the quarterback situation directly: "Greene, you're starting. Wilson, be ready. I plan to rotate you in every third series, plus specific situations. Both of you need to stay engaged, support each other, and be prepared to lead this team."

Tyler and Bear exchanged a nod of understanding. Over the past weeks, they had developed a rhythm of cooperation, each recognizing the unique strengths the other brought to the team.

The early tension of competition had transformed into a productive partnership that made the offense more versatile and unpredictable.

As the captains headed to midfield for the coin toss, Bear took a moment to center himself, to connect with the perspective he'd gained from learning Tony's full story. Whatever happened tonight—whether he played brilliantly or struggled, whether the team won or lost—the opportunity to touch the line would be there, in every decision, every interaction, every response to the inevitable adversity that playoff football brought.

Westlake won the toss and elected to receive. As the kickoff team jogged onto the field, Tyler approached Bear on the sideline.

"Remember spring workouts?" Tyler asked. "When we were both trying to prove we should be the starter?"

Bear nodded, remembering the intense competition of those early days.

"Look at us now," Tyler continued with a slight smile. "Co-quarterbacks in the state quarterfinals. Not how either of us planned it, but—"

"But maybe better than what we planned," Bear concluded, realizing the truth of it. "We've both grown more this way than if either of us had simply won the job outright."

Tyler nodded. "Iron sharpens iron."

The opening series set the tone for what would be a defensive battle. Westlake's first drive stalled after 3 plays against Jackson Creek's aggressive defense. When the Panthers' offense took the field with Tyler at quarterback, they found similar resistance, managing just one first down before punting.

The first quarter ended scoreless, with both defenses dominating. As the second quarter began, Coach Turner signaled to Bear: "Wilson, you're in. Let's see if we can change the tempo."

Bear jogged onto the field, his heart racing but his mind clear. In the huddle, he looked at his teammates, some showing fatigue, others frustration at the offensive struggles.

"One play at a time," he reminded them. "Trust the process. Execute."

His first pass was a quick slant to Akeem, who caught it cleanly and turned upfield for a 12-yard gain. The next was a designed quarterback draw that Bear took for another first down. Suddenly, the offense was showing signs of life.

But as they crossed midfield, disaster struck. Bear failed to see a safety rotating over on a deep throw, resulting in an interception that Westlake returned to the Jackson Creek 30-yard line.

Three plays later, Westlake was in the end zone. It was now 7-0.

On the sideline, Bear reviewed the intercepted play on the tablet with Tyler and the quarterback coach.

"Didn't see the safety rotate," Bear admitted, owning the mistake.

"We've all made that read before," Tyler said, in a surprisingly supportive way. "Shake it off. Next series will be better."

When Tyler returned to the field for the next drive, Bear remained engaged, studying the defense from the sideline, noting tendencies, identifying potential vulnerabilities. And when Tyler led a successful drive that ended with a game-tying touchdown just before halftime, Bear was the first to congratulate him as he came off the field.

"Great throw on that third down," Bear said genuinely. "Thread the needle."

In the locker room at halftime, with the score tied 7-7, Coach Turner's message was clear: "We're right where we need to be. Tied game against a team everyone expected to blow us out. But the next two quarters will be about mental toughness, about execution under pressure, about every man doing his job one play at a time."

He turned to the quarterbacks. "Greene, Wilson—both of you made some good throws, and both of you made mistakes. Keep supporting each other, keep learning from each series. We're going to need both of you to win this game."

The third quarter became a war of attrition. Neither team could establish consistent offense. Tyler led two series that resulted in punts. Bear's series gained momentum before stalling in Westlake territory, leading to a field goal attempt that sailed wide right.

As the fourth quarter began, Westlake put together their most impressive drive of the game, marching methodically down the field before punching in a touchdown. It was now Westlake 14-7, with 10 minutes remaining.

On the sideline, Coach Turner gathered the offense. "No panic. We've been here before. Execute the game plan."

He turned to Bear. "Wilson, you're up. Let's see what you can do."

In the huddle, Bear could feel the pressure of the moment—down 7 in the fourth quarter of a playoff game against a powerhouse opponent. His confidence suddenly faltered. The sheer weight of the moment closed in, threatening to cloud his judgment. But instead of letting that pressure distract him, he chose to embrace it. Tony's lessons about presence and inner strength flashed through his mind. "Pressure just means what I'm about to do *matters*," he told himself. He had struggled with these concepts before, but now he understood their true value. It wasn't about ignoring the pressure; it was about using it as a catalyst for focus and determination—to be fully present in this opportunity to lead.

Suddenly, he felt empowered. Pressure was his privilege—a privilege he wanted because it meant he was no longer simply reacting to the game; he was shaping it.

Taking a deep breath, Bear centered himself, his singular objective erasing the crowd noise from his mind.

"One play at a time," he told his teammates, his voice calm but intense. "This is why we practice. This is why we touch the line when no one's watching . . . for moments like this."

The drive began with a play-action pass that Bear delivered perfectly to the tight end for a 15-yard gain. Two running plays gained another first down. A screen pass picked up 12 more yards. The offense was finding its rhythm, moving steadily down the field.

At the Westlake 25-yard line, Bear recognized a blitz coming. He adjusted the protection at the line, then delivered a strike to Akeem on a slant route. Akeem broke a tackle and raced into the end zone. Touchdown. An extra point later, and it was 14-14 with 6 minutes remaining.

The Jackson Creek sideline erupted in celebration. As Bear jogged off the field, he was met by Tyler's outstretched hand.

"Clutch throw," Tyler said. "Perfect read on that blitz."

Bear nodded his acknowledgment, but his focus was already on the defense, willing them to get a stop and give the offense another chance.

The defense responded, forcing a three-and-out. As the Panthers prepared to receive the punt, Coach Turner approached Bear and Tyler.

"Decision time," he said. "Greene, you've been scheduled for the next series. But Wilson has the hot hand right now. What are your thoughts?"

The question hung in the air. Three months ago, it might have created tension. Now, Tyler didn't hesitate.

"Keep Wilson in," he said. "He's seeing the field really well right now. This is about winning, not about who gets the credit."

Coach nodded, seeming pleased but not surprised by the response. "Wilson, you're up. Make it count."

As Bear prepared to return to the field, Tony's words echoed in his mind: *The real victory won't be measured on the scoreboard, but in who you're becoming through the process.* Tyler's selfless response was evidence of his growth, his maturation as a teammate and leader.

Whatever happened in the next few minutes, that development was already a victory of sorts. But the game still needed to be won, and the next drive would likely determine the outcome.

With 4 minutes remaining, Bear led the offense back onto the field. The game plan called for a balanced attack to run clock while moving downfield. But on the first play, Bear noticed the safety cheating up, leaving vulnerability for a deep throw.

At the line, he changed the play: "Eagle! Eagle!" The offensive line adjusted their protection, and Bear took the snap, dropping back deep. The receiver ran a post route, breaking free of his defender. Bear delivered the ball with perfect touch, hitting the receiver in stride for a 45-yard gain.

Two plays later, the Panthers were in the red zone. But the Westlake defense stiffened, forcing a third-and-goal from the 8-yard line with 1:30 remaining.

Coach Turner called timeout and summoned Bear to the sideline. "What do you like here?"

Bear considered the defensive tendencies he'd observed throughout the game. "They're expecting pass. I think quarterback draw might work. They've been dropping eight into coverage on third down."

Coach nodded. "Do it. But if it's not there, protect the ball and we'll take the field goal to go ahead."

In the huddle, Bear called the play, noting the focused intensity in his teammates' eyes. "Quarterback draw on one. If it's not there, I'll get down. Ready? Break!"

At the line, Bear surveyed the defense, confirming they were indeed dropping eight defenders into coverage. He took the snap, feigned looking downfield, then tucked the ball and darted up the middle. The linebackers, anticipating pass, were too deep to close quickly. Bear burst through a gap and lunged for the goal line.

Touchdown. Jackson Creek 21, Westlake 14, with 1:22 remaining.

The Panthers' sideline and fan section erupted. As Bear jogged off the field, he was met by a wave of teammates, Tyler among them.

"One more stop," Tyler said above the noise. "Just one more stop."

The defense took the field with renewed energy. Westlake, now desperate, began throwing on every down. After two incompletions, they connected on a long pass that moved them into Jackson Creek territory.

The crowd noise intensified as the game entered its final minute. Westlake continued to march downfield, converting a crucial fourth down to reach the Jackson Creek 15-yard line with 12 seconds remaining.

On the sideline, Bear stood beside Tyler, both quarterbacks watching intently as their defensive teammates faced the defining moment of the season.

"They've got this," Bear said, partly to convince himself. "They've been clutch all year."

Westlake's quarterback took the snap, scanned the field, and fired toward the end zone. The Jackson Creek cornerback made a perfectly timed break on the ball, deflecting it away from the intended receiver. Incomplete. Eight seconds remained.

One final play. Westlake's last chance. The quarterback took the snap, evaded a rusher, and scrambled to his right, looking for an open receiver. He spotted one in the back of the end zone and released the ball just as a Jackson Creek defender hit him.

The pass sailed toward the receiver, who leaped to make the catch. For a heart-stopping moment, it appeared he had secured the ball. But as he came down, a Jackson Creek safety jarred it loose. Incomplete. Game over.

The Panthers had done the improbable—defeated Westlake to advance to the state semifinals.

The team stormed the field in celebration. Players, coaches, and even some fans formed a jubilant mass at midfield. Bear found himself embraced by his teammates and slapped on the helmet as he was pulled into the joyous chaos.

In the locker room afterward, Coach Turner could barely contain his pride. "That," he said, his voice thick with emotion, "is Jackson Creek football. Discipline. Unity. Resilience. Every man doing his job under pressure. Every man touching the line when it mattered most."

He singled out players for key contributions—the cornerback's deflection, the safety's game-saving hit, the offensive line's protection on the touchdown pass. And then he turned to the quarterbacks.

"Greene, Wilson—you two exemplify what this team is about. The way you've pushed each other, supported each other, made each other better—that's leadership. That's character. And tonight, it helped us beat a team that on paper should have dominated us."

As the team dispersed to the showers, still buzzing with excitement, Bear found a quiet corner to collect his thoughts. The game had been a validation of everything he'd been working toward, not just the victory or his individual performance, but the way he'd led, the way he'd maintained perspective, the way he'd executed under pressure.

Yet even as he savored the moment, he found himself thinking beyond the scoreboard, beyond the advancement to the semifinals. He was thinking about the growth he'd witnessed—in himself, in Tyler, in the entire team. About how the principles of touching the line, of finding the one-degree difference, had transformed not just their performance but their character.

His reflections were interrupted by Tyler, who had sought him out. "Heck of a game, Wilson," Tyler said, extending his hand.

Bear shook it firmly. "Couldn't have done it without you. That suggestion to Coach to keep me in for that last drive—"

"Was the right call for the team," Tyler interjected. "Three months ago, I don't know if I could have done that. But I've learned a few things this season."

"We both have," Bear acknowledged.

Tyler smiled slightly. "You think Tony planned it this way all along? Working with both of us separately, knowing we'd end up pushing each other to be better?"

Bear considered this. "Maybe. He's pretty wise that way."

"Pretty sneaky, you mean," Tyler corrected with a laugh. "But I'm glad he did it."

As they gathered their gear, Tyler added, "Whatever happens in the semifinals, this has been a hell of a season. Not the one either of us expected, but—"

"But better than what we planned," Bear said, echoing their pregame conversation. "Much better."

On the bus ride home, Bear's phone buzzed with a text from Tony: *Congratulations. You touched the line when it mattered most—not just in execution but in leadership. One more thing to remember: how you handle success is just as revealing of character as how you handle failure. Stay grounded.*

Bear smiled at the message, recognizing the wisdom in the reminder. Success could be as challenging a test as failure, in its own way. It would be easy to become complacent, to rest on this achievement rather than maintaining the discipline that had made it possible.

He glanced across the aisle where Max Jenkins sat, the freshman still buzzing with excitement despite not playing in the game. Max caught his eye and grinned.

"That quarterback draw was sick," Max said enthusiastically. "How did you know it would work?"

"Film study," Bear replied. "Noticed their tendencies on third down throughout the game. They consistently dropped eight into coverage."

Max nodded, absorbing this. "So it wasn't just a gut call. It was based on observation."

"Exactly," Bear confirmed. "The 'O' in COMPETE is *Observe*: Know the Rules to Win the Game. Understanding what moves the needle, tracking the right metrics. Do that consistently, and you start to see patterns others miss."

"Those frameworks really work, huh?" Max asked, a newfound respect in his voice.

"They really do," Bear assured him. "But only if you apply them consistently, not just when it's convenient."

It struck Bear that he was passing along Tony's wisdom in much the same way it had been shared with him—naturally, contextually, in moments when it could be immediately connected to experience. The cycle was continuing, the lessons rippling outward beyond their original source.

When Bear arrived home, his parents were waiting up for him despite the late hour.

"Congratulations, son," his father said, embracing him. "That was some game. The whole town is buzzing."

"We're so proud of you," his mother added. "Not just the winning touchdown, but the way you led out there. The poise, the teamwork, the character you showed."

Bear soaked in their praise, appreciating that it went beyond his athletic performance to the qualities that would serve him long after football was over.

"Thanks," he said simply. "It was a team effort."

"Get some sleep," his mother urged. "You look exhausted."

But despite his physical fatigue, Bear felt too wired to sleep. After his parents went to bed, he sat at his desk and opened his journal:

Today's Game: Performing under pressure in the biggest game of my life

My Competition: The temptation to make it about individual glory rather than team success

Why It Matters: Because touching the line in crucial moments is the ultimate test of character

What I experienced tonight wasn't just a football victory. It was a validation of everything I've been learning—about excellence, about leadership, about perspective. When Coach asked Tyler who should lead the final drive, and Tyler put the team above his ego . . . that was touching the line in a way that doesn't show up on statistics but matters more than any touchdown.

And in that moment before the quarterback draw, when everything was on the line, I felt a clarity I've never experienced before. Not anxiety, not pressure, but a calm certainty that came from knowing I'd prepared for this moment through thousands of small choices—all the times I touched the line when no one was watching, all the extra film study, all the mental reps.

Tony was right all along. The competition was never really about me versus Tyler. It was about both of us becoming the best versions of ourselves through the challenge we presented to each other. And in that becoming, we've both won, regardless of what the depth chart says or who gets more snaps.

As we prepare for the semifinals, I want to remember this feeling—not just the thrill of victory, but the deeper satisfaction of knowing we earned this through discipline, unity, and perseverance. And whether we win or lose next week, that transformation of who we've become is permanent. We've become a different team, different players, different people through this process. That's the real victory that can never be taken away.

Bear closed his journal, finally feeling the weight of the day's events settling into a profound fatigue. Yet as he prepared for bed, his mind was already turning toward the semifinals, not with anxiety but with a quiet confidence born of knowing he had touched the line in countless ways to reach this point.

Whatever came next—victory or defeat, starting or supporting, acclaim or criticism—he would approach it with the same discipline, the same perspective, the same commitment to excellence in the margins. Because that commitment had become not just what he did, but who he was.

And in that transformation from doing to being, Bear Wilson had discovered the ultimate purpose of touching the line.

CHAPTER 15
CHAMPIONSHIP CRUCIBLE

The December sky was overcast, steel-gray clouds promising winter's first real snow as the Jackson Creek team bus pulled into the massive NFL stadium for their state championship matchup. The enormity of the venue, with its 90,000 seats, massive video boards, and professional-grade facilities, made the occasion feel momentous from the moment they arrived.

Standing in the tunnel, waiting to take the field for warm-ups, Bear felt the weight of the moment settle on his shoulders. Not as a burden, but as an opportunity—the culmination of a season's journey, of countless small choices, of lines touched when no one was watching.

After defeating Jackson Creek in a blowout semifinal game the previous week, the team was ready for this final matchup. Unfortunately, they were down a man, with Tyler reinjuring his shoulder in the fourth quarter last week, sidelining him for the championship. Bear was now the undisputed starting quarterback. Coach Turner had been direct in his assessment: "This is your team to lead now, Wilson. You're ready."

The week of preparation had been intense but focused. Film study, practice reps, mental preparation, all approached with deliberate attention to detail. Central High, their championship opponent, was the defending state champion, undefeated in two seasons, with a defense that had allowed fewer than 10 points per game.

In the locker room before warm-ups, Bear found a moment of quiet. He opened his journal, adding a brief entry:

Today's Game: State Championship—the ultimate test of everything we've built

My Competition: The pressure of the moment and the temptation to make it bigger than it is

Why It Matters: Because this is where all the small choices reveal their impact

Whatever happens today, remember: It's still just one play at a time. Touch the line when it's hardest. The real victory is already secured in who we've become.

Bear closed the journal, centering himself in that truth. The outcome would matter—he was too competitive to pretend otherwise—but it wouldn't define him or the team's journey.

Tyler approached, arm still in a sling but dressed in full uniform. "Ready for this?" he asked.

"As ready as I'll ever be," Bear replied. "Wish you were out there with me."

"I am out there with you," Tyler said. "Maybe not physically, but everything we've built, everything we've learned—it's all part of today. And I'll be in your ear between series, seeing what you might miss."

Bear nodded, grateful for the support, for the partnership that had evolved from their initial competition. "Iron sharpens iron," he said.

"Until the end," Tyler agreed, extending his good hand.

Bear clasped it firmly.

Warm-ups passed in a blur, and soon the stadium was filling, the noise building as kickoff approached. In the locker room, Coach Turner's pregame speech was characteristically direct but charged with emotion.

"You've earned the right to be here," he told the team. "Not by talent alone, but through discipline, through unity, through touching the line day after day when no one was watching. Central High has the tradition, the rankings, the expectations. But you have something they can't measure or scout—the character you've built through this journey."

He looked around the room, making eye contact with each player. "Play free. Play together. Compete one play at a time. Trust your preparation. And whatever happens, remember who you are and how far you've come."

The game began with intensity, both teams executing at a high level. Central struck first, taking the opening drive for a touchdown. Bear responded with a methodical series that ended with a field goal. The score stood at 7-3.

The defensive battle continued through the first half, with Central adding another touchdown and Jackson Creek managing another field goal. At halftime, they trailed 14-6, still very much in the game but needing to find the end zone in the second half.

In the locker room, Bear huddled with Coach Turner and Tyler, reviewing plays, discussing adjustments.

"They're shifting their coverage post-snap," Bear observed, pointing to the tablet. "If we can catch them in transition—"

"Crossing routes," Tyler said, finishing Bear's thought. "Hit the seam during the rotation."

Coach nodded. "Good eye, both of you. Let's implement it the first series."

As the team prepared to return to the field, Bear gathered the offense.

"We're right where we need to be," he told them, his voice steady and confident. "They haven't seen our best yet. One series, one play at a time. This is what we've prepared for all season."

The third quarter began with Jackson Creek's most impressive drive of the game. Bear exploited the coverage shifts exactly as they had discussed, connecting on three crucial third downs. The drive culminated in a touchdown pass to Akeem, who made a leaping catch in the corner of the end zone. The 2-point conversion attempt failed, leaving the score Central 14-12.

The momentum shifted again as Central responded with another touchdown drive, extending their lead to 21-12 early in the fourth quarter. On the sideline, Bear could feel the pressure mounting, the opportunity slipping away.

In that moment, he recalled Tony's words: The real victory won't be measured on the scoreboard, but in who you're becoming through the process.

Bear gathered the offense again. "Nothing changes," he told them. "Our process, our standards, our execution. One play at a time. This is where champions touch the line when it's hardest."

The next drive displayed Bear's growth as a quarterback and leader. Despite the pressure, he remained poised, making reads, changing plays at the line, finding openings in the defense. The drive ended with another touchdown, narrowing the gap to 21-19 with 7 minutes remaining.

Central's next possession consumed valuable minutes but ended with a field goal. Now, it was 24-19 with just under 4 minutes to play.

As Bear prepared to lead the offense back onto the field for what might be their final possession, Coach Turner pulled him aside.

"This is the moment all those small choices have prepared you for," Coach said. "Whatever happens, I'm proud of you."

In the huddle, Bear could see the mix of determination and anxiety in his teammates' eyes. "One play at a time," he reminded them. "Trust the process. This is why we made the effort to go the extra inch when no one's watching."

The drive began with purpose, Bear connecting on short, high-percentage passes, moving the chains methodically. But at midfield, with just over 2 minutes remaining, disaster struck.

Bear's pass over the middle was deflected at the line and intercepted by a Central linebacker.

The Jackson Creek sideline fell silent. This was likely the end, barring a miraculous defensive stand. Bear jogged to the sideline, the weight of the moment crushing down.

Tony was waiting for him. "Look at me, Bear," he said, his voice cutting through the disappointment. "This isn't over. And even if it was, remember what game you're really playing."

Bear nodded, pushing through the emotions. "The bigger game."

"Exactly. Now support your defense. Be ready if we get another chance."

The defense took the field with renewed determination. Three plays later, they forced a fumble, recovered by Jackson Creek at their own 35-yard line. A glimmer of hope with 1:40 remaining.

Bear raced back onto the field, the momentum palpably shifting. The first play was a designed quarterback draw that Bear took for 15 yards. The next was a quick out to Akeem for another first down. They were moving, the Central defense suddenly on their heels.

At the Central 30-yard line with 45 seconds remaining, Bear recognized a blitz coming. He adjusted the protection, took the snap, and delivered a perfect throw to the tight end down the seam for a 25-yard gain.

First and goal from the 5-yard line. Thirty seconds remaining. The Jackson Creek section was in a frenzy, sensing the possibility of an improbable championship.

The first play was a fade to the corner that fell incomplete. The second was a run that gained 3 yards to the 2-yard line. Third and goal, 15 seconds remaining.

Coach Turner called timeout and summoned Bear to the sideline. "What do you like here?"

Bear considered the defensive tendencies he had observed throughout the game. "Slant to Akeem. They're expecting draw in this situation."

Coach nodded. "Do it. But be smart. If it's not there, throw it away and we'll have one more play."

In the huddle, Bear called the play, noting the locked-in focus of his teammates. "Okay . . . 400 Slants right on two. Akeem, sell the outside and cut in. If it's not there, I'll throw it away. Ready? Break!"

At the line, Bear surveyed the defense, looking for any indication they had anticipated the call. The linebackers were up on the line, the defensive ends in wide stances—all signs pointing to playing the run. He took the snap, feigned looking to his right, then turned to throw the backslide slant.

The opening was there initially, but then collapsed with surprising speed when a Central linebacker retreated. Instead of throwing it away, Bear sprinted around the left side to try and score with his legs. Reading the quarterback perfectly, that same retreating linebacker met Bear at the 1-yard line with bone-jarring force. Bear lunged forward, stretching the ball toward the goal line as he was driven backward.

The officials hesitated, conferring briefly before signaling: It was stopped short. Fourth and goal from the 1-yard line, 7 seconds remaining.

Coach Turner immediately called their final timeout. On the sideline, the tension was electric.

"One more play," Coach said. "We've come too far to settle for a field goal. What do you want to run?"

Bear thought quickly, replaying mental images of Central's goal-line defense. "Sprint right option. They'll expect me to keep it after that last play. Akeem will be open in the flat."

Coach looked to Tyler, who nodded agreement. "Let's do it. Trust your read."

In the huddle, Bear called the play, his voice steady despite the enormity of the moment. "Sprint right option on one. Primary read is Akeem in the flat. If they jump him, I'll keep it. Ready? Break!"

The teams lined up for the decisive play. Bear took a deep breath, centering himself in the moment. The snap came clean, and he rolled right as designed, scanning the field as the defense reacted.

Just as he anticipated, the defensive end crashed down hard, expecting Bear to keep the ball after the previous play. Akeem slipped into the flat, momentarily open. Bear cocked his arm to throw. But in that split second, a Central safety rotated over, jumping the route.

Bear pulled the ball back, looking for his secondary read in the corner, but the coverage was tight. With the defense closing in, he made a split-second decision—tucking the ball and cutting upfield toward the goal line, lowering his shoulder as two defenders converged.

The collision was violent. Bear felt himself driven backward but continued churning his legs, reaching the ball forward with every ounce of strength he possessed. For a moment, time seemed to slow as he felt the ball cross the plane of the goal line just before his knee touched down.

The official closest to the play hesitated, then threw his arms up: Touchdown!

The Jackson Creek sideline erupted. Players stormed onto the field, thinking they'd just won the state championship. But the celebration was premature. Another official was conferring with the head referee, who whistled for a review.

The stadium fell into a tense hush as the officials went to the replay booth. On the sideline, Bear stood with Coach Turner and Tyler, all three watching the giant video board as the replay showed different angles of the final play.

"Did you get in?" Tyler asked.

"I think so," Bear said. "But it's close."

The replay showed Bear's desperate lunge toward the goal line, the ball extended as far as his arm could reach. From one angle, it appeared to cross the plane before his knee touched. From another, it was maddeningly inconclusive.

Time seemed suspended, the entire stadium holding its breath. Bear's heart pounded in his ears, every second of the review stretching into what felt like minutes.

After what seemed like an eternity, the head referee emerged from the replay booth, turned on his microphone, and addressed the stadium: "After review, the runner's knee was down before the ball crossed the goal line. The play is ruled short of the goal line. Ballgame."

The Central side of the stadium erupted in celebration while a stunned silence fell over the Jackson Creek supporters.

The finality of it hit Bear like a physical blow. His legs buckled beneath him as he stood frozen on the sideline, his mind struggling to process what had just happened. All those months of work, all those early mornings, all those lines touched when no one was watching—all of it culminating in this moment where they had fallen literally inches short.

The scoreboard glared down mercilessly: Central 24, Jackson Creek 19.

In that moment, Bear felt a tide of emotions crashing over him—disappointment so acute it was almost physical pain, frustration that bordered on anger, a hollowness that seemed to spread from his chest outward. His vision blurred slightly, whether from exhaustion or the tears streaming down his face, he couldn't tell.

He stared at the field, replaying the final lunge in his mind. If he'd just stretched a little further, pushed a little harder, started his dive a split-second sooner . . . the what-ifs threatened to drown him.

Around him, the reactions of his teammates told their own story of heartbreak. Some collapsed to their knees having played their final career game, others stood in shock at how close they were to winning. A few even turned away, unable to watch the Central celebration. Three years of high school football, countless hours of practice, all the sacrifices . . . and they had fallen just short.

Coach Turner's hand on his shoulder broke through his shock. "Head up, Wilson," he said, his voice steady but thick with emotion. "That's not how competitors respond."

The words cut through the fog of disappointment, reaching something deeper in Bear. He took a deep breath, forcing air into lungs that felt constricted with grief, wiped his eyes, and straightened his shoulders.

In this crucible moment, when it would be so easy to collapse under the weight of defeat, to lash out in anger, and to make excuses, Bear felt something crystallize within him. A

DRIFT INTO BITTERNESS OR DIRECT HIMSELF TOWARD SOMETHING BETTER.

choice presented itself with perfect clarity: drift into bitterness or direct himself toward something better.

The Competitor's Choice. Here, now, when it mattered most.

Bear nodded, swallowing hard against the lump in his throat. He looked Coach Turner in the eye, then deliberately scanned the sideline, making eye contact with his devastated teammates. They were looking to him now, watching how he would respond.

With deliberate steps, Bear moved toward the handshake line, his posture tall despite the crushing weight in his chest.

"Let's go, guys," he called, his voice stronger than he expected. "We finish this right."

As the team gathered for the post-game handshake line, Bear led the way, making sure to look each Central player in the eye, offering sincere congratulations despite the raw wound of disappointment still bleeding inside him.

The walk across the field felt like the longest of his life, each step requiring a conscious decision to move forward, to honor the game, to be the person he had been becoming all season . . . especially now, when it was hardest.

This, Bear realized through the haze of disappointment, was the ultimate line to touch: the one between character and collapse, between who you are when you win and who you are when you lose everything that seems to matter.

And in that extra inch, in making that choice when it would have been so easy to drift, Bear understood that something important remained undefeated, even if the team was not.

In the locker room afterward, the atmosphere was heavy with emotion, some players openly crying, others sitting in stunned silence, a few angrily slamming lockers. Bear recognized the pivotal moment this represented, not just for him but for the entire team.

Before Coach Turner could speak, Bear found himself standing.

"Guys, listen up," he said, his voice steady despite the emotion behind it. "This hurts. It *should* hurt. We came so close."

He paused, gathering his thoughts. "But this game—this season—was never just about a championship trophy. It was about who we became through the process . . . about the small choices we made every day that transformed us as players and as people."

Looking around the room, Bear continued, "Today doesn't erase any of that. We're still the team that outworked everyone, that competed hard when no one was watching, that transformed from a collection of individuals to a true brotherhood."

Tyler joined him, standing despite his injured shoulder.

"Wilson's right," he said. "We've all experienced something here that goes beyond wins and losses. We've learned what it means to compete with each other instead of against each other. To go the extra inch to touch the line when it's hardest. Those lessons don't disappear because we came up short today."

Coach Turner stepped forward, his eyes reflecting both pride and the sting of defeat. "I couldn't have said it better myself. What you just heard from these two young men—that's true leadership. That's character revealed in the crucible of disappointment."

He looked around the room, making eye contact with each player. "Yes, we lost the game. But in the things that truly matter most—discipline, unity, perseverance, and character—this team is undefeated."

After the coach's words, the atmosphere in the locker room subtly shifted. The disappointment remained, but alongside it grew a sense of perspective, of pride in what they had accomplished and who they had become.

As the team began to disperse, Bear found a quiet corner to change. Tony approached, sitting beside him.

"How are you really doing?" Tony asked quietly.

Bear considered the question honestly. "Disappointed. Hurting. But also . . . determined, somehow. It's strange: I wanted that championship so badly, but right now I'm thinking about what this means for next year, for the team I'll be leading as a senior."

Tony nodded. "That's wisdom, Bear. That's growth. Most people never learn to see beyond the immediate disappointment to the lessons and opportunities ahead."

"I keep thinking about your story," Bear admitted. "About how your struggles ultimately taught you more than your early success did. And I realize, I have a whole senior season to apply what I've learned here."

THE REAL TEST OF CHARACTER ISN'T WHETHER YOU WIN OR LOSE; IT'S HOW YOU RESPOND TO BOTH.

"Exactly," Tony said. "This isn't an ending, Bear. It's preparation. Everything you've learned this year—about leadership, about character, about competing with instead of against your teammates—that's all preparation for what you'll face as a senior captain."

He looked Bear directly in the eye. "The real test of character isn't whether you win or lose; it's how you respond to both. Tonight, you showed these guys how to handle defeat with dignity.

"Next year, you'll get to show them how to channel disappointment into determination."

"The Competitor's Choice," Bear said, understanding.

"Always," Tony confirmed. "In victory or defeat, the choice remains the same: drift or direction, default or desired. And now you get to help an entirely new group of players understand that choice."

As they gathered their gear to leave, Tony had one final thought: "Bear, what happened tonight doesn't define you

. . . it *refines* you. You're going to be a different kind of senior leader because of this experience. And that might be worth more than any trophy."

In the days that followed, the pain of defeat gradually softened, though it never fully disappeared. Bear found himself returning to his journal daily, processing the experience, extracting lessons, preparing for what lay ahead:

Today's Game: Processing defeat while preparing for future leadership

My Competition: The temptation to dwell on what could have been rather than what still can be

Why It Matters: Because how I respond to this will shape the kind of senior leader I become

The championship game taught me that even when you do everything right—touch all the lines, make all the right choices, prepare thoroughly—the outcome isn't guaranteed. There's always an element beyond your control.

But what remains entirely within my control is how I respond and what I do with this experience. This isn't the end of my story; it's the end of one chapter and the beginning of another. As a senior next year, I'll have the chance to take everything I've learned and help build something even stronger.

The one-degree difference applies here too. The gap between water and ice exists in defeat just as it does in victory. And choosing direction over drift is perhaps even more important now as I prepare to lead others.

A week after the championship game, Coach Turner called a final team meeting. When the players gathered in the locker room, expecting a season wrap-up, they were surprised to find a table full of small boxes.

"Before we close this chapter," Coach began, "I want to give each of you something to commemorate this season."

He opened one of the boxes, revealing a silver keychain in the shape of a football with "THE EXTRA INCH" engraved on one side.

"This phrase has become the heartbeat of our program this year," Coach continued. "It represents the countless small choices each of you made daily—in practice, in the weight room, in the classroom, in life—that transformed not just our team, but each of you individually."

He began distributing the boxes, calling each player by name. When he reached Bear, he paused.

"Wilson, you didn't just embrace this concept, you helped spread it throughout our team, our school, our community. Next year, as a senior, you'll have the opportunity to build on this foundation and take our program even further."

As Bear held the keychain, turning it over in his hand, he noticed something on the back he hadn't seen from a distance—the date of the championship game and a single word: "FOUNDATION."

Coach Turner finished handing out the keychains, then addressed the team one final time:

"A foundation is what you build upon. This season was our foundation. It tested us, challenged us, and ultimately prepared us for what's next. Disappointment and adversity can either become the dirt that buries us or the cornerstone we build upon.

"For our seniors, remember these lessons as you move forward. For our returning players, use this foundation to build something even stronger."

After the meeting, as players dispersed, many sought out Bear—to talk, to thank him, to acknowledge how his example had influenced them.

Max Jenkins was among them.

"So, what now?" Max asked. "After coming so close?"

Bear considered the question. "Now we build on what we learned. Keep competing. Keep touching the line and going that extra inch. This season ends, but our development never does . . . it just moves to the next level."

Max nodded, understanding dawning. "So this was preparation for next year?"

"Exactly," Bear acknowledged. "Everything we went through this year—the lessons, the growth, even this disappointment—it's all preparation for what we can become as seniors and leaders."

As winter settled over Jackson Creek, the football season faded into memory, but its lessons became the blueprint for what was to come. Bear continued meeting with Tony regularly, their conversations now focused on senior leadership and the culture he wanted to build.

One snowy afternoon in January, as they sat in the local coffee shop, Tony posed an important question: "Have you thought about what kind of senior leader you want to be next year?"

Bear considered this carefully before answering. "I used to think leadership was just about being the best player. Now I know it's about making everyone around you better. I want to create a culture where every player understands what we learned this year . . . that the real competition is with yourself, that excellence is built in the small moments."

"That's good," Tony said. "Because you have a unique opportunity. You've experienced both the heights and the disappointment. You understand what it takes to build character through adversity. That's exactly what next year's team will need."

Bear nodded, understanding more deeply now. "Like what you've done with me and Tyler. And what I started with Max . . . but on a bigger scale."

"Exactly," Tony said. "And the beautiful thing is, you're already doing it. Max is different because of your influence. Other players are embracing these principles because they've seen how they transformed you."

He smiled, adding, "Next year isn't about winning back what you lost—it's about building something even better."

As Bear walked home through the gently falling snow, he reflected on the season's journey—from frustrated backup to team leader, from narrow ambition to broader purpose, from seeing the championship as the ultimate prize to understanding that the real victory lay in who he was becoming and who he could help others become.

The state championship trophy might not be in Jackson Creek's case yet, but something more valuable had been secured—a foundation of character, of perspective, of understanding what truly constituted excellence. And that foundation would serve as the cornerstone for what they could build next year.

In his journal that night, Bear made a simple entry:

Today's Game: Preparing to lead rather than just perform

My Competition: The expectation that senior year is about individual achievement

Why It Matters: Because the most meaningful leadership happens when you elevate others

I'm beginning to understand what Tony has been teaching me all along. The championship game wasn't the end of the journey—it was preparation for the next phase. Everything I learned this year as a junior—about character, about competing with teammates instead of against them, about touching the line when it's hardest—now becomes the foundation for how I'll lead as a senior.

This disappointment has actually given me something valuable: the perspective to know that winning isn't just about the scoreboard. It's about building something that lasts beyond any single season. Next year, I'll have the chance to help create that with a new group of players.

That's the true championship opportunity ahead. And unlike a trophy, what we build in character and culture can never be taken away.

CHAPTER 16
SEASON'S END, NEW BEGINNINGS

Spring had arrived in Piney Creek, bringing with it the promise of new beginnings. Bear stood on the empty football field, the afternoon sun warm on his face as he finished his workout. The stadium was quiet now, a stark contrast to the roaring crowds that had filled it during the championship run just four months earlier.

He closed his eyes, remembering that final drive, that last desperate lunge toward the goal line that had come up just inches short. The sting had faded, replaced by something more valuable—perspective, determination, and a clear vision of what his senior year could become.

In the months since the championship game, Bear had processed the disappointment, celebrated the team's accomplishments, and continued applying Tony's principles to every area of his life. His chemistry grade had finished strong with an A-, a testament to his consistent work with Heather. More importantly, he'd been officially named team captain for his senior season—a role that carried far more weight and responsibility than any starting position ever could.

"Thought I might find you here," a familiar voice called.

Bear turned to see Tony approaching from the sideline, carrying his usual clipboard and water bottle. They still met regularly, though their sessions had evolved from basic skill development to advanced leadership preparation.

"Just visualizing," Bear replied with a smile. "Thinking about what we want to build next year."

Tony nodded, understanding. They walked together to the 50-yard line, the spring breeze carrying the scent of fresh-cut grass and possibility.

"How's the college recruiting process going?" Tony asked.

Bear had been receiving increased attention from college programs after his junior season performance. Several Division II schools and a few smaller Division I programs had extended scholarship offers—solid opportunities that balanced football with academics.

"Getting closer to a decision," Bear replied. "State University feels right. Strong business program, offense that fits my style, and close enough for family to visit. But honestly, I'm more focused on this senior season than what comes after."

"Good perspective," Tony said. "Present moment focus while keeping future goals in sight." They walked in comfortable silence, each processing the significance of this transition period.

"You know what's different now?" Bear said finally. "Last spring, I was obsessed with just making the varsity team, proving I deserved a chance. Now I'm thinking about how to build a championship culture, how to develop the younger guys, how to leave this program better than I found it."

"That's leadership maturity," Tony observed. "Understanding that your role extends far beyond your individual performance. You're thinking like a captain now, not just a player."

Bear nodded, recognizing how profoundly his perspective had shifted. "The game really is bigger than football. It's about becoming the kind of leader who elevates everyone around him, who creates standards that outlast his own involvement."

"Exactly," Tony replied, genuine pride evident in his voice. "And you're already demonstrating that. The work you've been doing with Max Jenkins, the middle school quarterback camps, the way you've embraced the mentorship role—that's leadership in action."

"Tyler's doing well at Texas A&M," Bear mentioned. "Says the frameworks we learned here have been crucial for his adjustment to college ball. He's competing for significant playing time as a freshman."

"That's the ripple effect," Tony said with satisfaction. "The principles you both internalized are serving you beyond this field, beyond this town. And now you get to pass that same gift to the next generation."

Bear appreciated how the influence had spread—from Tony to him and Tyler, from them to younger players, and soon to an entirely new senior class he'd help lead.

"I've been thinking about what kind of captain I want to be," Bear admitted. "Not just someone who gives speeches or leads drills but someone who embodies what we learned this year .

THE BEST LEADERS DON'T JUST TALK ABOUT STANDARDS—THEY LIVE THEM SO CONSISTENTLY THAT OTHERS CAN'T HELP BUT BE INFLUENCED.

. . someone who shows others what it looks like to compete every day, to touch the line when it's hardest."

"That's wisdom beyond your years," Tony said. "The best leaders don't just talk about standards—they live them so consistently that others can't help but be influenced."

They walked back toward midfield, their conversation shifting to Bear's specific plans for the upcoming season—team-building initiatives, mentorship programs, and the culture he wanted to establish from day one of summer workouts.

"You know," Tony reflected, "when I first called you out for not touching that line during your sprints, I saw potential. But what you've become exceeds even what I hoped for. You've developed into someone who doesn't just pursue excellence—you inspire it in others."

"I owe that transformation to you," Bear said sincerely. "That moment changed everything—not just my football approach but my entire understanding of what it means to compete and excel."

Tony smiled. "That's how mentorship works. Someone plants seeds, but you did the growing. You took those principles, made them your own, and now you're ready to plant seeds in others."

As they reached the sideline, Bear noticed Max Jenkins and a few other underclassmen running conditioning drills on the track. Max spotted them and jogged over, his respect for Bear evident in his approach.

"Bear! Good to see you," Max called out. "We're working on that footwork progression you showed us. Starting to feel more natural."

"Excellent," Bear replied, studying Max's posture and confidence. "Remember, consistency in the small details creates consistency in the big moments."

"Absolutely," Max said, nodding his head in agreement. "Hey, are we still on for that leadership session this weekend? Some of the guys who'll be juniors next year want to join."

Bear felt a surge of satisfaction. "Definitely. Bring whoever wants to learn. We'll talk about what it really means to lead a team."

As Max rejoined his workout, Tony chuckled. "You see that? You're already functioning as a mentor, a teacher, a leader. That young man looks up to you the same way you looked up to me."

Bear reflected on this observation. "It's humbling. And motivating. I want to give him the same gift you gave me—not just football skills, but a framework for approaching challenges and competition in every area of life."

"That's exactly what true leadership looks like," Tony confirmed.

As they walked toward their vehicles, Bear felt a profound sense of purpose about the year ahead. Senior year wouldn't just be about personal achievement or even team success—it would be about building something lasting, creating a foundation that would serve the program long after he graduated.

"Whatever this senior season brings," Bear said thoughtfully, "I'm grateful for everything I learned as a junior. The disappointment, the growth, the perspective—it all prepared me for what I need to do as a leader."

"That's the beauty of these principles," Tony replied. "They prepare you not just for immediate challenges, but for responsibilities you can't yet imagine. Everything you've learned about competing with yourself, about touching the line, about choosing direction over drift—it all becomes the foundation for how you'll lead others."

At their cars, Tony extended his hand, but Bear pulled him into a brief hug.

"Thank you for believing in me," Bear said.

"The honor was mine," Tony replied. "But remember, this next chapter is just beginning. You have an entire senior year to demonstrate everything you've learned, to build something special, to leave a legacy that extends far beyond any individual season. And I'm here to help any way I can."

Bear nodded, understanding completely. The principles he'd internalized, the character he'd developed, the perspective he'd gained—these would now be tested in the crucible of senior leadership. The lines worth touching would multiply, but his commitment to touching them would remain unwavering.

As he drove home, Bear felt a quiet confidence about the year ahead. Senior year would bring new pressures, new expectations, and new opportunities to either drift toward mediocrity or direct himself and his teammates toward excellence.

But he was ready. More than ready. The real game was just beginning.

In his journal that night, Bear wrote:

Today's Game: Preparing to lead others toward excellence

My Competition: The temptation to focus on personal achievement over team development

Why It Matters: Because senior year is my opportunity to multiply the impact of everything I've learned

Junior year taught me what it means to compete with myself, to touch the line when it's hardest, to find the one-degree difference that transforms performance and character. Now I get to help others discover these same truths.

The championship game showed me that the scoreboard doesn't always reflect the real victory. The real victory is in who you become through the process, and who you help others become along the way.

Senior year isn't just about fulfilling my own potential—it's about unlocking potential in others, creating a culture of excellence that outlasts any individual season, touching lines that create ripples extending far beyond what I can see.

That's the ultimate competition. That's the line worth touching above all others.

EPILOGUE
BEYOND THE GAME

As the sun set over Jackson Creek, casting long shadows across the football field, Max Jenkins completed his final sprint. He bent down, deliberately touching the line at the far hash mark, just as Bear had taught him.

It had been three years since that first summer when a skeptical freshman had met the backup quarterback who would change his approach to not just football, but life itself. Now, as the starting quarterback heading into his senior year, Max was carrying on the legacy Bear had passed to him.

On the sideline, Bear Wilson watched with approval. Home from college for the summer, he resumed his role as mentor, though the relationship had evolved into more of a partnership as Max had grown in both skill and maturity.

"You've got a good one there," Tony said, joining Bear on the sideline. "Reminds me of someone else I used to know."

Bear smiled. "He's come a long way. Not just as a quarterback, but as a person." He paused, then added, "I had a good teacher."

Tony nodded appreciatively. "The best teachers are the ones who become unnecessary. He doesn't need you hovering over him anymore."

"No," Bear agreed. "But we all need reminders sometimes. The line is always there, waiting to be touched."

As Max jogged over, Bear could see the changes three years had wrought—not just in physical development, but in the confidence that came from discipline consistently applied, from challenges met, from incremental growth compounding over time.

"How'd I look?" Max asked, wiping sweat from his brow.

"Sharp," Bear replied. "Your footwork on the five-step is more consistent. No wasted motion."

Max nodded, taking the assessment seriously. "Been working on it. That extra split second makes a difference in the pocket."

"One degree," Tony observed with a smile.

"Exactly," Max agreed, clearly familiar with the concept. "Water to ice."

As they gathered their equipment, Max asked Bear about his college season.

"Challenging," Bear admitted. "Being redshirted was harder than I expected. All practice, no games. But it gave me time to learn the system, bulk up, get faster. Coach says I'll be competing for the backup job this fall."

"You'll get it," Max said with certainty. "You always win the game that matters."

Bear glanced at Tony, both of them recognizing the echo of their earliest conversations. The vocabulary of competition had spread, the frameworks extending to a new generation.

"State championship this year?" Bear asked Max, changing the subject.

"That's the plan," Max replied. "We've got the talent. But talent's not enough."

"What else?" Tony prompted, though he knew the answer.

"Discipline," Max said without hesitation. "Consistency. The small choices no one sees that compound over time. Touching the line when it's hardest."

Bear felt a surge of pride, not in his own influence, but in Max's internalization of the principles. The freshman who had once thought he could get by on natural ability alone had become a senior who understood that excellence was built in the margins, in the extra inch, in the one-degree difference.

As they walked toward the parking lot, Max said offhandedly, "I've been working with some of the middle school quarterbacks. Teaching them the frameworks, the journal process, all of it."

"How's that going?" Bear asked.

"Good," Max said. "They're like sponges at that age. And explaining it to them helps me understand it better myself."

Tony nodded. "Teaching is the highest form of learning."

In the parking lot, Max said his goodbyes and headed home, leaving Bear and Tony alone in the gathering twilight.

"Full circle," Tony observed.

"It's strange being on the other side of the relationship," Bear admitted. "Watching him grow, knowing I played some small part in it."

"Not so small," Tony said. "You put effort into something that created ripples beyond what you could see. That's how legacy works."

Bear considered this. "I never thought about legacy when I was in high school. I was just trying to win the starting job, get better, maybe earn a scholarship."

"Most people never think about it," Tony agreed. "They focus on immediate outcomes—trophies, positions, titles. But the true champions understand they're building something that outlasts those momentary achievements."

They reached their cars, a familiar scene that had played out countless times over the years—mentor and mentee, teacher and student, now colleagues in a shared mission of developing excellence in others.

"You know," Tony said as he unlocked his truck, "the story's never really over. The line is always there to be touched or missed. The one degree is always waiting to transform water to ice. The question is whether we make The Competitor's Choice—day after day, moment after moment."

Bear nodded, understanding more deeply with each passing year. "That's what makes it both challenging and beautiful, isn't it? The game never ends. We just keep finding new lines to touch, new ways to go the extra inch further."

"Exactly," Tony confirmed with a smile. "And that's why the journey itself—not just the destination—matters so much."

As they parted ways, Bear thought about all the lines still waiting to be touched in his life—college football, academics, future career, relationships, community. The specifics would change, but the principles would remain the same.

He thought also about the legacy that had been passed to him and that he was now passing to others—the understanding that excellence wasn't an event but a habit, that character was revealed in the small choices made consistently over time, that the most important competition would always be against one's own potential.

In that legacy, in that transmission of wisdom from one generation to the next, in that commitment to finding the extra inch in every pursuit, Bear Wilson had discovered a purpose larger than any individual achievement—to be a link in a chain of excellence that extended far beyond himself.

And as he drove away from the field where his journey had begun with a missed line and a mentor's challenge, he carried with him the certainty that the most important lines to touch still lay ahead—not on any athletic field but in the quality of life he would build, the impact he would have, the example he would set.

That was the ultimate line worth touching. That was the one-degree difference that truly transformed everything.

That was the extra inch that made all the difference.

NOTES

Chapter 3: Touching the Line

1. Albert Camus, *The Myth of Sisyphus and Other Essays,* trans. Justin O'Brien (New York: Vintage International, 1955), 123.

Chapter 4: The Cheated Rep

1. Marty Smith, *Sideline CEO: Leadership Principles from Championship Coaches* (New York: Twelve Books, 2023), 71–72.

RESOURCES TO HELP YOU MEET *THE LINE*

If you want to enhance your reading experience, visit www.GoTheExtraInch.com to:

- Watch videos on concepts from the book.
- Grab a free 'Book Club Discussion Guide' to take your team/group through.
- Learn strategies to implement the *COMPETE* frameworks in your playing, academic, or professional career.
- Find posters and products with key quotes from *The Line*
- Order wristbands for your players, team, or organization.
- Get additional resources that will help you go the extra inch to compete every day.

BRING *THE LINE* TO YOUR TEAM AND ORGANIZATION

If you are interested in helping your team learn how to compete every day, contact our team at:

Phone: (945) 348-0271

Email: Booking@CompeteEveryDay.com

Online: CompeteEveryDay.com OR JakeAThompson.com

Instagram | TikTok | YouTube: @JakeThompsonSpeaks

Sign up for weekly *Beat Yesterday Playbook* email at Lead.CompeteEveryDay.com

To purchase bulk copies of *The Line* at a discount for large groups, athletic departments, or your organization, please contact our team at Team@CompeteEveryDay.com.

ABOUT THE AUTHOR

Jake Thompson knows what it's like to feel stuck between good and great.

As a leadership performance coach and chief encouragement officer at Compete Every Day, Jake has spent over a decade discovering that the principles separating elite performers from everyone else aren't complicated—they're just consistently applied.

But it wasn't always that way.

Jake's journey began in 2011, selling T-shirts out of the trunk of his car with a simple belief: **your biggest competition is you.** What started as a grassroots movement has now reached leaders in over sixty-two countries who've discovered that excellence isn't about perfection—it's about the daily choice to compete against yesterday's version of yourself.

Through his work with over 85,000 ambitious leaders and organizations worldwide, Jake developed the proven **COMPETE** framework that helps high achievers close the gap between knowing what to do and actually doing it. His insights have been featured in *Forbes* and *Inc. Magazine,* and his podcast has generated over two million downloads from leaders seeking that extra edge.

Jake's credentials include:

- MBA and Mental Performance Master (MPM) Certification
- CSP® (Certified Speaking Professional)—earned by only 17 percent of speakers globally through the National Speakers Association
- Over a decade of entrepreneurial sales experience and client work

When he's not coaching leaders or writing, you'll find Jake in Dallas/Fort Worth with his wife, Elena, and their four rescue dogs: Sugar, Donut, Snacks, and Pop-Tart—who teach him daily lessons about unconditional enthusiasm and living in the moment.

Jake's mission remains simple: Help you win the most important game you'll ever play—the daily competition against your own excuses, distractions, and tendency to settle for "good enough."

Because every day, you get to choose: drift or direction. This book will help you choose wisely.

To Learn More and Find Out How You Can Work with Jake & His Team, visit **www.JakeAThompson.com**